HOW WE HEAR

HOW WE HEAR

How Tones Make Music

by

MAX F. MEYER

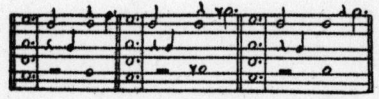

CHARLES T. BRANFORD CO.

Boston, Massachusetts

COPYRIGHT 1950
by
MAX F. MEYER

Printed in The United States of America

FOREWORD

I have here summarized my work of fifty years in acoustics and music, scattered over thirty articles in scientific magazines in both German and English, taking into account recent discoveries. The reading, done slowly, should take about four hours. It requires no mathematical knowledge beyond what one learns in a secondary school. The book is addressed to acousticians, otologists, theorizing musicians, teachers of speech correction, teachers of the deaf, and laymen interested in general science.

The functions of the brain, and in general the *neurological* aspects of audition, are not discussed in the present book. The reader interested in them is referred to Ernest G. Wever's book, *Theory of Hearing*, (1949). However, all the *important mechanical theories* of the cochlea hitherto proposed are reviewed in the first part of the latter book as an introduction to the neurology. Professor Wever on page 88 says of my mechanical theory, what he says of none of the others, "Meyer's theory has received far less consideration than it deserves." He adds, "It is a difficult theory: difficult in conception and perhaps more so in its presentation . . . It has a number of outstanding merits . . . It is indeed ingenious in its conception of a mode of analysis without recourse to resonance."

Ever since Helmholtz in 1862 published the first edition of his book, *Die Lehre von den Tonempfindungen,* (*The Sensations of Tone* in its English edition), almost every acoustician adopted as the basis of his reasoning the idea that the cochlea was a kind of musical instrument performing for the brain as its audience. Through the medium of the sound-conducting air a sympathetic (literally!) relation was thought to establish itself between the outside instruments, as in the orchestra, and that imaginary musical instrument within the head, and the relation thus conceived was the answer to the problem, "How our brains hear." During the succeeding years a great many modifications of the original version of Helmholtz were published, as reviewed by Wever. But they all agreed that the cochlea was a vibrating musical instrument. Only two authors disagreed, Pierre Bonnier and Max Meyer. The former failed to elaborate his dissent.

When as a student I devoted myself to physiological acoustics, I could not help rejecting the grossly mythological notion of a sympathetic sense organ making music for the brain. Trained in mathematical physics, I could not see the *physical* possibility of pendulum-like vibrations within the cochlea, since its anatomy had already become fairly known. In 1896 I conceived a mathematical analysis of the compound sound waves brought to the ear which discarded all sinusoidal vibrations within the cochlea. I published it. A German physiology professor reviewing it called the idea "childish." That did not discourage me. In 1898 I published the mechanical counterpart to the same mathematical analysis. Reviewers of acoustical literature did not read my publications with enough care to avoid reading into them their own notions instead of mine and either left my ideas totally unmentioned or mentioned them so distortedly that I could not recognize as my own the ideas presented as mine.

Not long ago in a letter to me Professor Wever wrote: "I can appreciate your feelings on this matter after reading all the curious statements about it in the literature. I have not found a single one anywhere that does justice to your ideas, and most of them are so wrong that it is apparent that the authors have not read your writings, but have satisfied themselves by reading one another's versions and so perpetuating one another's errors. From experience I have learned not to trust secondary sources. It is amazing how often they are wrong."

I decided then to present my conception of the hydraulic-mechanical functioning of the cochlea, free from all hypotheses of masses, tensions and the like not justified anatomically, summarily in an easy—indeed semi-popular though not unscientific—style. So I wrote the present book, which I hope will appear less formidable than my previous publications.

The theory of music presented in the later chapters has no direct connection with the theory of the cochlea. In this respect, too, I differ from Helmholtz, who based his theory of music upon his own theory of the cochlea. Until the beginning of the twentieth century all musical theory was dominated by the idea of Rameau that the essence of all music was found in the two chords called major and minor, and that the three inversions of each alike constituted the diatonic scale, so-called. In my book, *The Musician's Arithmetic*, (published by the University of Missouri and now obtainable from Theodore Presser, Philadelphia), I have shown the historical and scientific origin of Rameau's ideas and also the fallacious conclusions which he drew from them. The composers of the twentieth century have freed themselves from the restraint of Rameau's dogma. The real basis of a psychologically correct theory of music I have summarily described in the last chapters of the present book.

Miami, Florida   M. F. M.

CONTENTS

Chapter		Page
I	What May Happen When A Straight Tube is Shaken	3
II	What May Happen In A Curled Tube	8
III	What May Happen In A Doubled-Up Tube	11
IV	What Will Happen If The Direction Of Shaking Is The Inutile (Unprofitable) Direction Between P and N In Figure 3	14
V	What Is Accomplished By A Leathery Wall Dividing The Doubled-Up Tube Into Two Halves	15
VI	How Violently Must The Skull Be Shaken For An Auditory Effect?	20
VII	What Kinds Of Air Puffs Are There?	23
VIII	How The Ear Drum Aids In The Perception Of Rather Low Tones	27
IX	Where And What Are The Sensitive Cells	32
X	The Thesis, The Parathesis And The Hyperthesis Of The Phragma; And The Safety Valve	36
XI	On What Cochlear Conditions The Perceived Loudness Of A Tone Sensation Depends. Also First Discussion Of Analysis Performed By The Cochlea	42
XII	Masking Seemingly Obvious (In A Theory Too Simplified) But Actually Abated By The Hyperthesis Intervening	49

Chapter		Page
XIII	Two Kinds Of Beats: Unison Beats Multiple Frequency Beats	54
XIV	The Tones Of Tartini	62
XV	Asserted By Some Authors, But Non-Existing Tones Of Tartini	69
XVI	Another Example Of A Tartini Tone	73
XVII	Computation Of Ordinate Differences	80
XVIII	Summary Of The Function Of The Cochlea. Deafness	83
XIX	The Greatest Discovery In Music	86
XX	The Two Aspects Of A Melody: Pitch Changes And Melodious Affinities	89
XXI	Another Sample Of A Musical Scale	97
XXII	Frozen Melodies. Symphonic Music. The Possibilities Of Quartertones	104
XXIII	A Rational Script For Music	112

HOW WE HEAR

Chapter I

WHAT MAY HAPPEN WHEN A STRAIGHT TUBE IS SHAKEN

Deeply imbedded in the thick bone which forms the base of the skull are two little tubes, one on each side of the head, which serve as the sense organs of hearing. Contrary to what would seem to be the more natural shape, the tubes are coiled and not straight. When one scrapes away the somewhat spongy bone surrounding, one finds that each tube is coiled up much like the shell of a garden snail. For this reason the customary name for the tube, during hundreds of years, has been "the snail". The anatomists, speaking an international language derived from the Greek, have given it the corresponding technical name of "cochlea," and under this scientific name we shall hereafter often refer to it. The fact that the tube is coiled up has no functional significance and might be explained by saying that during the evolution of the mammalian family of animals, Nature thus found room more easily for it in the base of the skull. We shall, in these pages, speak of the cochlea as if it had been unrolled.

It is essential, as we shall see, that this vessel be rather long: a real tube, that is, long and thin. In animals lower than the mammalian group such as birds and reptiles, (whose sense of hearing is simple—in spite of the singing characteristic of birds), the tube is so short as to hardly deserve the name. It forms no snail shell. The size of the total "snail" in a human being, let us add, is about that of a cherry.

Someone might at once ask the question, "But why does the coiling not interfere with the functioning of the tube as a sense organ? Remember how blurred our vision becomes when during sleep, sometimes, temporary pressure on the eyelids causes the eye-ball to be even slightly misshapen!" That, however, is quite a different matter. The fundamental principle in this little tube, we shall later see in detail, is chiefly the minute back-and-forth movements lengthwise in the tube of the liquid contained therein; and such movements of the liquid do not require the tube to be straight. Think of how little the curves of the plumbing in our house interfere with the flow of the water.

Speaking of minute lengthwise movements of liquid in any tube, we are obliged to ponder the question, "How can such movements of the liquid be produced?" In order to answer this question with perfect freedom from all prejudices with which the older technical literature abounds, it is best to forget for awhile all about the cochlea as well as about physical tones in acoustics, and to make a few simple experiments with a straight tube, say, a thin-walled, straight lead pipe, which we can hold in our hands. Take such a lead pipe a few feet long both ends of which are closed exactly with light corks, yet loosely fitting and very well lubricated. Before we insert the second cork, fill the pipe completely with water. Let us hold the pipe horizontally, so that gravity, the attraction of the earth, will not prevent the water from remaining in the pipe. We can then move the pipe in our hands, as long as we keep it horizontal, without fear that any water will escape, provided our movements remain very, very gentle.

Fig. 1. A lead pipe filled with water. Keeping it horizontal means that all the arrows remain on the plane of this page.

Now make a movement far from gentle, a jerky movement, in the direction from A to B in Figure 1, that is, in the direction from your left shoulder to your right shoulder. According to the physical law called "inertia" the liquid in the pipe tends to stand still while the pipe is being jerked to the right. The result is that, relative to the pipe, the liquid tends to move in the direction from B to A. Thus you will observe as the consequence that the left cork has been pushed slightly outward and the right cork has been sucked slightly inward.

If the motion of your arms had been extremely violent, you would even observe that the left cork had been driven out of the pipe completely. But such violence is not a necessary part of our further thinking.

One must make it perfectly clear to oneself that the flow of the liquid is not an emptying flow like that of the water in our house piping, during which all the water in the right part of the tube might flow all through the length of the tube. The flow of the liquid which we are considering here is only a flow through an extremely small distance; and after that all the liquid remains again at a standstill.

If now you make a jerky movement of the pipe in the direction from your right shoulder to your left shoulder, all the other directions are reversed too. That is, the right cork is pushed slightly outward and the left cork is correspondingly sucked inward.

Now consider what would happen if you moved the pipe jerkily forward from your chest, in the direction from C to D. According to the laws of physics nothing whatsoever could result in the water; and both corks would retain exactly the position which they had before you jerked the pipe forward from your chest. But that would be true only if the motion occurred exactly in the direction C-D forming a right angle with the pipe. If you jerked the pipe even a little slantingly, deviating from the angle of ninety degrees even much less than the direction E-F in Figure 1 indicates, the result would be some flow of the liquid and some motion of the corks.

We shall later understand that such a jerky back and forth movement of the liquid in the tube is the very foundation of the functioning of our sense organ of hearing. That being so, we naturally ask if a jerky motion of the tube by an external body which shakes it is the only way in which such a motion of the liquid within the tube can be induced. Immediately we observe that it can also be induced in a different way. Again take your lead pipe filled with water which is kept from running out by the two light and lubricated corks. Now press very gently upon one of the corks with your finger. Naturally you produce the same kind of jerky motion of the liquid lengthwise in the tube which we have discussed. If you take the end of the corked pipe in your mouth and suck a little, you move the corks and the water back to where they were before. If the corks are well lubricated and you have pretty strong lungs, even a puff of air against one of the corks could produce the effect spoken of. That the resulting motion might be so slight as to be unnoticeable to the naked eye, is no objection to our reasoning, for the motion of the liquid in the human sense organ always remains of microscopical measure.

Chapter II

WHAT MAY HAPPEN IN A CURLED TUBE

We asked you to imagine a lead pipe with walls so thin that we might easily straighten it out or bend it at will in our hands.

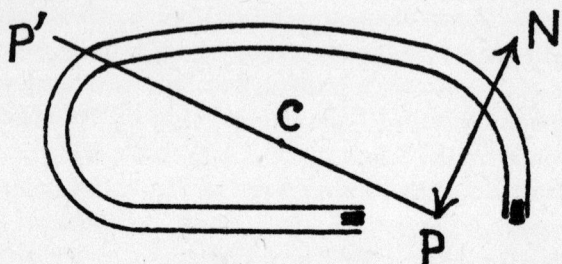

Fig. 2. A curled lead pipe filled with water.

Now let us bend the tube into the shape shown in Figure 2. Then let us give this curled tube a jerk, but just as before, keeping every part of the tube within the plane indicated on these pages. In almost every direction of jerking the results would be the same which are described above as occurring in the straight tube. The corks would slightly slide opposite in the sense of one in, one out. That is, one would be sucked by the water, the other would be pushed. There is a single direction in which the jerking may occur without producing any result. If we jerk the curled tube in this direction, either of N-P or of P-N in the tube system of Figure 2, nothing will result. Just a few minutes of thinking will tell us the nature of the direction of the line N-P. Freezing the water in the tube and at the same time evaporating the lead walls is of course physically impossible. Nevertheless, imagine for a moment that it was done. Now hold the page in this book vertically and imagine you were rotating the frozen, curled rod of water as the garage man rotated the wheels of your motor car when you asked him to "balance" the wheels. Complying with your request he equilibrated the wheels so that when he left any wheel alone, it would not begin to rotate spontaneously; that is, he weighted the different points of the periphery of the wheels so that the center of weight, technically called "the center of gravity," would be *identical* with the center within the bearings around which which the wheel is forced to rotate by the engine. In our curled, frozen rod of water of Figure 2, C is the center of gravity of this rod of water. And P is a point midway between the ends of the frozen rod; or, in an experiment, P is the point midway between the ends of our curled tube. We draw P-N vertical to P-P', or as the mathematicians say, "normal", to P-P', the latter line passing through the center of gravity C.

If you now jerk our curled, water-filled tube in the direction P-N or N-P, nothing can happen to the liquid. Neither of the originally placed corks will budge, provided you do not deviate in the least from the direction given by the normal P-N on P-P'. It takes a certain amount of mathematical training to understand why the direction of P-N is mechanically determined exactly in this way. The average reader not having that training will probably rather take on faith what anyway will appear plausible to him, (that there must exist such an exceptional direction!), than be bothered by the strict geometrical proof. Therefore we omit here the latter.

In life, of course, if there is any shaking at all, the complete avoidance of deviating from the directions P-N or N-P would be as rare as the finding of a needle in a haystack.

As with the straight tube in Figure 1, so here in Figure 2: you could also produce a slight lengthwise motion of the water in the tube by gentle pressure of your finger applied to either cork. Or you could do it by sucking either end of the tube. Or you could do it by applying a strong enough puff of air blown from your lungs against either end of the tube.

Chapter III

WHAT MAY HAPPEN IN A DOUBLED-UP TUBE

Let us experiment a little further with our water-filled tube as shown in Figure 2. We squeeze it together until it appears doubled-up as in Figure 3, taking care that the one end remains a certain distance, A-B in the figure, from the other

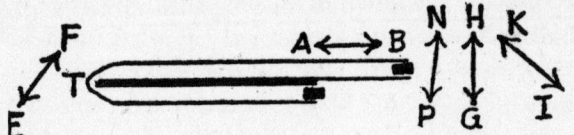

Fig. 3. The tube is squeezed and doubled-up.

end, just as the two ends appeared apart in Figure 2. We squeeze the parallel lengths together until they flatten against each other, so that where the two "halves" touch each other, they form together something like a single tube divided into halves by a partition or "phragma." This latter term is common in biological science. Henceforth we shall always call this partition "the phragma of the cochlea." In Figure 3 it is indicated by the thick division line from A to T.

Now to continue our experiment. Let us empty our lead pipe and then cut out and replace the flattened and doubled wall piece by a strip of very soft leather, such as chamois skin. The leather is held in place by no particular force. It is held in place, in addition to "floating," merely by the wall edges left unaltered and lying against each other with the leather between them. A particular warning must be issued against imagining any stretching, any "tension" of the leather strip. The leather at rest there is in no way stretched. If it were stretched, we should *lose all the analogy* existing between this tube system and the snail which is the sense organ of hearing. Anatomical investigation has proved that the phragma is *free from tension at rest*. Now we fill the tube again with water and put the lubricated corks again in their proper places.

You shake the tube of Figure 3 either in the direction between E and F or in the direction between G and H (which is normal to the phragma) or in the direction between I and K. In all such cases you force a jerky flow of water between the cork B in the figure and the cork below A. But since the flattened "metal" has been replaced by very soft "leather," *between* A and B now no longer signifies *by way of* T to A. The soft and possibly flabby leather (compare Figures 6 and 7) now goes with the jerky *flow of water neatly "around" the corner* at A. There is only one direction of shaking which will *not* bring about any such flow. You can *not* bring about any flow when you shake the tube system in the direction between P and N, which is now almost but not quite parallel to G-H, because the center of gravity lies now only a very minute distance above the phragma. Consequently the former P-N of Figure 2 must now form almost a right angle with the phragma.

Perhaps puzzled we ask the question, "What happens in the two halves *together* of the doubled tube between near-A and T (*not* B and T) when we shake the tube system of Figure 3?" The answer is simple. Nothing happens! The soft and flabby leather just acts like anything *floating* in the water; and the whole *double* tube between that corner not distant from A and the far region at T is simply a "dead end street" in which no flow is possible lengthwise or crosswise no matter in which direction we shake the tube, — — unless by shaking it *powerfully* we bring into operation quite a new factor (a strong reciprocating motion of the column between A and B) as we shall see in Chapter V and further on.

As in Figures 1 and 2, so here in Figure 3 the same effect may be produced if, instead of *shaking* the tube system, we simply *puff* alternately against the corks. If after one we puff against the other cork, we bring both corks back to where they were originally; or if we puff against the latter a little harder, we bring the former even beyond the place where it was originally, that is, make the cork at first pushed-in now stick-out a little: and the reverse concerning the other cork. Important observation: *shaking or puffing* are the two modes in which Nature normally, mechanically stimulates the organ of hearing, that is, *sets in reciprocating motion the liquid column between A and B.*

Chapter IV

WHAT WILL HAPPEN IF THE DIRECTION OF SHAKING IS THE INUTILE (UNPROFITABLE) DIRECTION BETWEEN P AND N IN FIGURE 3

Imagine that you are playing the role of the Creator and that you have progressed as far as we have here with the problem of designing a sense organ of hearing; and now you become aware of the fact that there is a certain, though very restricted, *direction* in which the hither-thither *shaking* of the tube system is as profitless as would be any *simultaneous puffing* against *both* corks.

Since cases like that in reality would be very rare indeed, you would not give up your engineering problem as hopeless. Suddenly it would occur to you that it is only necessary to furnish the living being with *two* sense organs located so that neither one could ever be in the unfortunate compass range at a moment when the other one happens to be there. And in this manner Nature has solved that problem. What in this circumstance we can not hear with one ear, we have a chance to hear with the other. Just as a bird, which has one eye on either side of the head, often sees with one eye what it can not see with the other eye.

Chapter V

WHAT IS ACCOMPLISHED BY A LEATHERY WALL DIVIDING THE DOUBLED-UP TUBE INTO TWO HALVES

A person endowed with some curiosity must ask the question, "Why is there a soft leathery wall between the two halves of the whole tube in Figure 3 from the region A and the cork there, on the one hand, to the point T on the other hand?" Since lengthwise movements of the water in this "dead end street with a parking between the traffic lanes" seem to be excluded, what is the use of that "parking," the phragma, at all? We shall give the answer.

We have already convinced ourselves that jerky back and forth movements of the "water rod" located between A and B in Figure 3 are induced either by shaking the whole tube system or by puffing against one or the other "cork." Near A the water goes *around* the corner and takes from the placement indicated by the line at *a* in Figure 4 a *short* length of the leather with itself to placement *b,* without tearing the leather, if the water motion is very minute and the leather practically floats. That is, the water motion is very minute *as long as the* external forces are small enough. Although these external forces, shaking or puffing, are always of very small absolute magnitude, even small things can have a great variety of magnitude, as one easily learns by familiarity with a microscope. If now the lengthwise motion of the "water rod" located between the cork under A and the cork at B becomes relatively somewhat *more* forceful, will it still, while going around that corner near A, take that *same short length* of leather further down with itself? The answer must be a conditional "No!" Nature *must* have seen to it that there is a limit to the up and down displacement of the phragma because the contents of the phragma, delicate hair cells, would be ruined by an excessive displacement, which involves shearing.

When the force of the water's motion around that corner at A increases, the leather near that corner soon resists and virtually (we shall later see "not absolutely") stops yielding. But the *force* of the "water rod" located between A and B still grows toward the maximum (or minimum) of the pressure curve! What then? Well, a little piece of the leathery wall *next to* that nearest short length now yields, bulges, so much *lengthening* the first bulge until this additional length of the phragma comes to a virtual stop, too. Then a further little piece yields until it comes to a stop, too. And so forth. Let us assume, in order to have something definite to speak of, that *the last yielding* point of leather is located

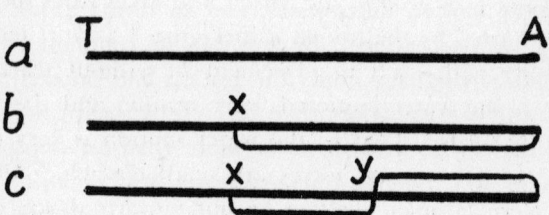

Fig. 4. The force of the water pressure from the right of A grows, then is reversed with the temporary result shown.

at the point x leftwards from A in Figure 4*b*. That means, the positive outside force has become zero. Now let us assume that the water column between A and B in Figure 3 under a *negative* outside force reverses its motion and flows to the right. Then the force applied at the point A on the phragma is negative, of the nature of *suction*. With the suction force increasing, further and further little pieces of the leathery phragma are moved up, *each until* it virtually resists the hydraulic pressure and stops moving up. Figure 4 quite arbitrarily is drawn as if the suction force had *exhausted itself* to zero when the upward jerking of the phragma had reached point y. Of course, the suction force may not yet be *spent*, not until point x is reached or even a point farther to the left from x. That detail is not under discussion at this moment.

It would be a grave misunderstanding if any one should try to speak of these up or down motions of the points all along the phragma in Figure 4 as *vibrations*. Each of these motions is a jerky motion downwards (like those in Figure 4*b*) followed by a rest period and then followed by a jerky motion upwards (Figure 4*c*); then possibly again by a rest and a jerky motion downwards, and so forth. That is *not* what one calls vibrations. By a *vibration*, common language and technical language imply the restless and smooth motion of a point in one direction, then the reverse, again the reverse of that, and so forth, with never more than an *infinitesimal* moment of rest, that is, no measurable rest at all. A true vibration is exhibited by a pendulum. A pendulum is not jerked from one side to the other, then after a while jerked back, and so forth. Therefore we must *not* speak of the down and up movement of the phragma illustrated in

Figure 4 as a *vibration* of any point of the phragma. Nothing "vibrates" there. "Jerks" of the successive phragma points is the proper term.

Suppose now that in our experiment described at the point y the external force is exhausted: the water column between A and B immediately stands still. What then becomes of the strange positions of the phragma as shown at b and at c in Figure 4? For a little while hardly anything will be seen to happen. By "a little while" is meant in the present paragraph something like two or three seconds or any duration of that order of magnitude. Then the phragma, if free from all external influence, will slowly (perhaps only in ten or fifteen seconds) reassume the "normal" position which is indicated by the line corresponding to a in Figure 4.

Now we can give a preliminary answer to the question, "What is accomplished by all this?" In detail the answer will be given in the later chapters. Here we merely satisfy the physicist who refuses to postpone his desire to see the action of the external force quantitatively related to the magnitude of the internal energy consumption. The greater the external force, the greater the extent of motion of the liquid column located between A and B in Figure 3. When this column is pushed inward, a *part* of it passes beyond A to the left. We might even say that it "sheds" a piece of itself. Room must be found for what is shed; and room is made in the depression, or bulge, seen between A and x in Figure 4 at b. There is equality between the extent of motion of the column A-B and the room made within this bulge. The longer the bulge, the more liquid it can receive. However, instead of speaking of a longer bulge, we may as well speak of a greater length of a phragma piece reacting. Chapter IX will make clear that the *length* of this phragma piece is what concerns us.

The ends of the tube have been given two distinct names in anatomy. The end at B is called the oval window, that at A the round window. Compare Chapter VII.

When an air puff reaches the round window and the liquid column A-B then moves to the right in Figure 3, it naturally *sucks into itself* a certain quantity of liquid, which must come from the upper bulge A-y of Figure 4 at c.

To the mathematical physicist I say emphatically that I avoid the term "amplitude" when speaking of the extent of motion of column A-B in Figure 3, because "amplitude" might suggest, even can not help suggesting a "sinusoidal vibration." The *form* of the motion of the column A-B is here entirely irrelevant. The later chapters will have to say more about that.

Chapter VI

HOW VIOLENTLY MUST THE SKULL BE SHAKEN FOR AN AUDITORY EFFECT?

How extraordinarily small a force is needed to be applied in shaking the skull to produce the motion of the liquid located between A and B in Figure 3 is most remarkable. Nature here has long preceded the inventions of the communication engineers by which they magnify minute causes acting, say, on the antenna of a radio into grand effects. Take into your hand an ordinary watch which is ticking. The action of the tiny escapement within makes the whole watch tremble. But the sense of touch of your hand is incapable of telling you that your watch is trembling, that it is running or has stopped.

Suppose you are in a perfectly soundproof room. Now press the watch against your upper teeth. At once you hear the ticking because the trembling watch shakes the skull sufficiently in spite of the enormous difference of weight of the two bodies. It is analogous to the Moon making the Earth tremble and causing tidal waves which you can see, but which, while sitting on your chair at home, you do not feel.

Suppose you are a singer getting ready to sing before an audience. In order to be sure of the pitch with which you start, you carry a tiny tuning fork hidden in your hand, but you do not want the audience to know that you are going to use it. Inconspicuously you make it vibrate so softly that neither the other people nor even you can hear the tone. Now behind a seemingly accidental movement of your hand you bring the foot of the vibrating tuning fork in touch with one of your upper teeth; and at once your skull is shaken sufficiently to make you hear clearly the desired pitch.

The designers of so-called "hearing aids" for those who are hard of hearing have manufactured little telephone receivers no larger than a lady's wrist watch. The hard of hearing person hangs the contrivance over one of the gristly flaps which everyone of us carries at the sides of his head and which we curiously enough call our "ears." The telephone receiver itself is made to touch the protrusion which one has behind the "ear" because it is very inconspicuous there and also because the skin is thin there and does not act much as a cushion on the bone of the skull. When now the microphone which the same person carries in a pocket or elsewhere on the body, is excited, the telephone receiver gently "hammers" the bone and thus shakes the whole skull, with the result on the tube system which we have discussed.

The medical doctors who specialize in curing defects of hearing call themselves "otologists," because "otion" is one of the Greek words for ear. For more than a hundred years the otologists have accustomed themselves to speak of "bone conduction hearing" when they meant hearing brought about by shaking the skull. The phrase is not a very happy way of referring to the facts. It makes one think of "a thing conducted" by the bone to the sense organ. As a matter of fact the sense organ, the shell of which we have described as a tube system, is an intimate part of the bone of the skull, not something separate from the skull and waiting for the skull to carry something to it. When the skull is shaken, the tube system is shaken. That is all to be said about it.

Chapter VII

WHAT KINDS OF AIR PUFFS ARE THERE?

Stimulation of the auditory organ through shaking the skull is for animals living on and above the surface of the earth less common than stimulation through air puffs. The reverse may be true for mammalians who live in the water and keep their heads more or less submerged, as seals. Before we discuss the air puffs, let us now in our thinking do away with the lubricated corks closing the two ends of the tube system. In reality the opening under A in Figure 3 is closed by a delicate membrane which is called by the anatomists the membrane of the "round window." The opening at B is not round but oval. It is not so simply closed by an ordinary membrane but, for reasons which we shall understand later, by a combination of a ring-shaped membrane with a plate. The central space of this membranous ring is filled by the bony plate which the anatomists call "the plate of the stirrup." The end of the tube at B where the stirrup plate is found is called the "oval window" in order to speak of it in distinction from the "round window."

Air puffs which can act on the windows (alternately on either as we shall see) may be produced very easily in the following manner. Take a disk about a foot in diameter, of metal or thin wood or cardboard, and punch or drill out in a circle any number of holes an eighth or a quarter of an inch in diameter. Locate the end of a little pipe made of glass or any other material opposite a hole. Rotate the disk on a central axle and blow through the pipe. The air puffs originating on the other side of the disk propagate themselves to your ear, that is to the windows spoken of, and you have the sensation of a tone. If the disk is rotated faster, there are more air puffs per second and the pitch heard is higher. If the rotation is slower, you hear a lower pitch. How this comes about will be explained later in detail.

Such "siren" puffs prove that puffs acting on the "windows" do *not* have to be of the nature of air pressure smoothly waxing and smoothly waning as one might imagine when one sees the *smooth* curves which illustrate most books on acoustics. The puffs may be each quite abrupt and yet cause the desired tone to be heard. The so-called "air wave" of the *puff* is propagated through the outer ear canal, which is called by the anatomists the "auditory meatus;" it is as little interfered with by the ear drum as is the piano concerto performed in the next room separated from yours only by a paper wall, and passes with virtually no interference through the so-called "middle ear," a cavity not filled with a liquid but with air. This air pressure wave passing the middle ear then reaches B in Figure *3 before* it reaches A.

The water column between B and A is incompressible. That is, all physicists agree that water is compressed with such difficulty that in comparison with air it must be regarded as incompressible. Accordingly, *just as soon* as the puff pushes the oval window at B inwards, this water column, B-A, also pushes the round window outwards, a little while *before the air puff* has reached the round window. The result is something which was already pictured at *b* in Figure 4. A certain length of the phragma has been pushed down, until the puff at B has spent its force; these details were described in Chapter V.

A little while later, that is, a very small fraction of a second later, the pressure of the propagated puff reaches the point A, that is, the round window. The result is something like what is shown at c in Figure 4, although the point y is likely to be identical with the point x (which, however, is immaterial at this moment). Thus the piece of the phragma between A and y (or x) is jerked (one down plus one up movement *counting as one jerk*) as many times per second as disk holes of the rotating siren have passed the blow pipe per second.

Air puffs may result from innumerable other causes. For example, thunder is a series of very strong but rather irregularly succeeding air puffs. The roar of a cannon, the sound of a pistol shot are other instances of irregular air puffs.

The air puffs which we use for producing with musical instruments the perception of music are almost always of the smoothly waxing and waning kind. Rare kinds of percussion instruments might be cited as rare exceptions. The smoothness results from the fact that musical instruments are *vibrating* elastic bodies, either *stretched* strings or *real volume* bodies like the air bodies inclosed in flutes and organ pipes or the solid bodies of the xylophone or bells or gongs or triangles, etc. The voice sounds made by human beings, cows, dogs, cats, etc., are also mostly composed of smoothly waxing and waning air puffs because they result from elastic cushions, wrongly called vocal "chords," which obstruct intermittently the passage of compressed air from the lungs. However, the effects on the sense organ are exactly the same, whether the air puffs acting on it are abruptly starting and abruptly ending ones or smoothly waxing and waning air puffs. The alternating air pressures acting on the sense organ by no means have to have the form of the motion of a pendulum, which is called by the physicists a sinusoidal motion or a vibration. The motions within the cochlea, the reactions of any particular point of the phragma, are never true vibrations; they are nothing but up and down jerks in any case. There are no sinusoidal motions, pendulum-like motions, in the phragma, since the latter has no permanent tension, not being stretched in any way.

Chapter VIII

HOW THE EAR DRUM AIDS IN THE PERCEPTION OF RATHER LOW TONES

It is clear that the membranes closing the two windows of the cochlea at A and B in Figure 3 must be kept as flexible as possible. Therefore, whenever the outside air happens to be very dry, it should be kept away from them. It would also be a disadvantage if insects could freely crawl into the outer air canal, proceed and reach the windows and possibly do harm to them. To serve both these protective needs Nature has put the ear drum, called "tympanum" by the anatomists, across the air canal, the "meatus." We have already pointed out that the passage of air puffs is in no way obstructed by this very thin wall. The air puffs pass beyond it virtually as if the tympanum did not exist.

We must now recall, as a basis for further understanding of our sense organ, the speed with which any kinds of air waves propagate themselves in an air room. This has been found by the physicists to be something more than 1100 feet per second, or, we may say, more than 13,000 inches per second. What one calls the length of an air wave is the distance from the point where the pressure is a maximum to the point where the pressure is again a maximum. In the middle of the wave length is the pressure minimum. The wave length depends on the frequency with which the waves or "cycles" follow one another. Imagine a tone where this frequency is 100 cycles per second; the wave length of the tone then must be one hundredth of 13,000 inches, must be in the neighborhood of 130 inches. For the greater frequency of 1000 it would be only 13 inches. Now imagine the frequency of a very high tone, say, the frequency 10,000 which is much beyond the limits of a grand piano; the wave length then must be in the neighborhood of one and one-third inches. Such rather short wave lengths are easy for the cochlea to take. Not so any very long wave lengths, as we shall see below.

In Figure 3, for the sake of clearness of appearance, the distance *between* the windows at A and B is somewhat overdrawn. On the real cochlea it is *barely a quarter of an inch*. How great then is the *fraction* of the pressure difference of an air wave *effective* on the windows? To get a clearer answer to this question, we use the sketch of Figure 5.

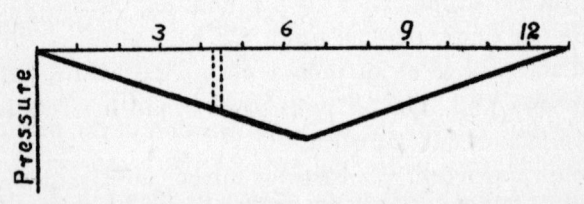

Fig. 5. The *drop* between the dotted lines stands for the *active* pressure difference between the windows.

Take the case of a wave frequency about 1000 which belongs neither to an exceptionally high nor to an exceptionally low tone. The wave length in air then is 13 inches, as already stated. That is too long a distance to be shown on the page of this book. Therefore imagine the 13 spaces of Figure 5 to stand for the 13 inches of the wave length. The one-fourth of an inch from B to A on the outside of the cochlea then would be represented by the small distance between the dotted lines. The amount of drop (or rise) between these dotted lines would show what a *small fraction only* of the air wave's maximum pressure difference, indicated by the depth of the triangle, would be utilized in order to move the water column located between the points A and B in Figure 3. The relative smallness of this useful fractional pressure difference may appear surprising. But we remember how great the sensitiveness of the sense organ was found to be when we shook our skull by merely holding a running watch against our upper teeth. A frequency of 1000 is not yet so low, the wave not yet so long, that the cochlea could not take it without any difficulty.

But now let us contemplate the wave length of a much lower tone than 1000, say, of the cycle frequency of 100 only. To find then the *utilizable* fraction of the maximum pressure difference, we have to divide the wave length in Figure 5, not into 52, but into 520 parts. Then the drop (or rise) of the pressure line within one of these 520 parts of the wave length would indicate the utilizable fraction of the maximum pressure difference of the air wave of 100 cycles per second. This drop is too small to be shown in Figure 5 by dotted lines. It means a great deal to expect that amount of sensitivity from the cochlea. Nature better do something about it to help matters along!

Well, Nature has done something about it. The tympanum, we noted, primarily provides two different kinds of protection. Why not assign to it a third role? Does not the roof of our house serve more purposes than the single one of shedding the rain? It also furnishes shade. Moreover, it protects the rooms of the house against the cold of the sky. In like wise the tympanum. Also, a third function is assigned to the ear drum. It is only necessary to *connect the tympanum solidly* with one window, that is, with the plate of the oval window, either by means of a *rod* as in the birds, or by anything serving likewise as in the mammals.

Turning again to Figure 3 we recognize that now the utilizable pressure difference within the air wave is no longer limited to the small air distance from B to A, but is extended to the greater air distance from the location of the *tympanum* to the location of the round window at A. The air puff on reaching the tympanum *already* pushes B inwards and A simultaneously outwards.

This alone increases the effectiveness of the *push* to three or four times of what it would be otherwise. (By the way, physicists have determined that the *pull* of the tympanum on the human stirrup plate is relatively ineffectual. The tympanum here works with a slight approximation to a rectifying vacuum tube.)

An even greater advantage is obtainable by attaching this connecting rod to the tympanum under a rather small angle. The effect there is that of using a lever. Those readers who are interested sufficiently in that part of the problem, will find it discussed in detail in almost every book on anatomy.

It goes without saying that the *musician* must also help by producing the tones of *low cycle frequency* with very big and *powerful instruments,* conspicuous in the orchestra or band. Little and weak instruments, too, can be built so that they vibrate only a small number of times per second, but their tones would not be audible.

We spoke of a rod connecting the drum with the oval window in the birds. In mammals, we find instead of a solid rod, a jointed combination of three solid bodies, the so-called "ossicles," having the fantastic names of hammer, anvil and stirrup. They serve in the same way in which the bony rod serves in the birds.

That this solid connection between the oval window and the protective tympanum is not an essential feature but only an auxiliary arrangement, becomes clear when we read the otologists telling us that those of their patients who have lost the tympanum together with the ossicles, are by no means necessarily deaf. They can still hear, but not as well as before.

Chapter IX

WHERE AND WHAT ARE THE SENSITIVE CELLS

In higher animals the nervous system, or as we usually say singling out its most massive part, the brain, can be affected for its normal functioning only under rare circumstances in a direct manner. Almost always it is necessary to act on mediators called sensitive cells. From the latter certain processes of an electro-chemical nature then proceed to and through the *brain*.

In the cochlea the sensitive cells are located all along within the phragma. But they are located there "looking toward" one side only. Let us call that side in our illustrations the "upper" side. They are not standing there in a single file. Rather they appear like a queue of people waiting to be admitted to a place through a door broad enough for three or even five persons to pass abreast, shoulder to shoulder. They count up to many thousands. When a thin slice is cut from the tube crosswise and examined under the microscope, one usually sees there from three to five sensitive cells side by side. These cells are several times as tall as they are wide. On the end opposite to the end on which they are standing, they carry a little brush of hairs, and for that reason they are often called the "hair cells." Over them floats a very delicate membrane barely touching the hair cells so that the hairs may brush this membrane when the bottom part of the phragma, usually called the "basilar membrane," which supports the hair cells, is jerked in a particular region in the manner which we have described.

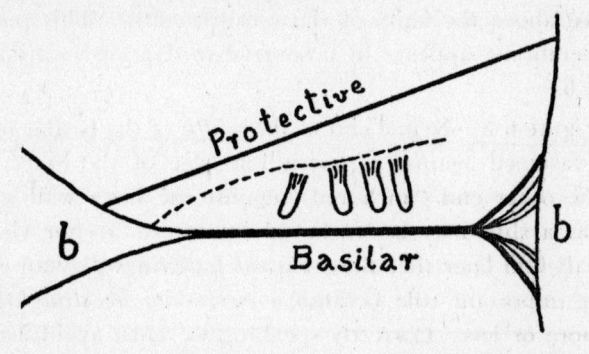

Fig. 6. At b and b is the bony wall forming the spiral shell of the cochlea. The floating membrane is shown dotted.

A certain *protective* membrane within the cochlea still needs to be mentioned. When a piece of the phragma, say, at the point x in Figure 4, is jerked from one position to another, it is the result of hydraulic pressure. But the latter results from minute but relatively violent motions of the liquid *lengthwise in the tube* both above and below the length between A and x. In the sketch of Figure 6, which is a cross-section of the doubled tube, we see the hair cells and the delicate membrane, indicated by a dotted line, against which the hair cells probably brush. The minute but violent motions of the liquid aforementioned occur below and above the phragma, though vertical to the plane of these pages. The bottom part of the phragma, which is the relatively tough basilar membrane, cannot be harmed by these motions of the liquid. But above, at the floating membrane, the hair cells need protection from the *friction* of the liquid moving vertically to the plane of these pages. Nature therefore has placed a protective membrane a little distance above the hairs of the sensitive cells. This protective membrane appears in a somewhat slanting location in Figure 6.

In Figure 6 we see one end of the *width* of the basilar membrane fastened against a protruding edge of the bony wall and the other end "anchored" against the bony wall somewhat as a ship may be anchored by *curved* anchor chains. We shall find later that these *curved fastenings* play an enormously important role because *a curve can be straightened out,* more or less. Correctly speaking we must avoid a common error of parlance which means by "phragma" only the basilar membrane; we must include everything located between the protective membrane and the lower surface of the basilar membrane as shown in Figure 6.

What now is the physico-chemical nature of the hair cells? Modern neurological research has definitely proved that the hair cells function like piezo-electric crystals used in radio communication. The Greek word "piezo" means literally "squeeze." Certain natural objects, especially the crystals of certain minerals, have the property of becoming electrically charged when they are ever so slightly squeezed; and because of this property they are widely used in the construction of microphones and for broadcasting of whatever frequency is desired. When the hairs are distorted, the hair cells of the cochlea are electrically charged. The hairs are distorted in consequence of the phragma being jerked. The number of charges per second is the same as the number of jerks per second. These charges are then transferred to the auditory nerve and charges of the same frequency pass through the brain. We then hear a higher tone when the frequency is greater, a lower tone when the frequency is smaller.

Of course, why we are *conscious* of anything when electric charges pass through the brain is a metaphysical question which Science can not answer. Science restricts itself to describing as plainly and as accurately as possible that which goes on in physico-chemical Nature.

Chapter X

THE THESIS, THE PARATHESIS AND THE HYPER-THESIS OF THE PHRAGMA; AND THE SAFETY VALVE

In Figure 4 the phragma, which *in reality* is not a simple leather strip but *quite complex* as we have seen in the previous chapter, is represented by a single line. That is a great advantage when we intend to study the deformation of the phragma. These deformations show up so much more clearly in a thin line than they would in a picture like Figure 6. So we return here to speaking of the phragma as if in a cross-section of the tube it were a simple line. It is very important, however, to keep in mind that in purely "mechanical" functioning the basilar membrane is the most *important* part of the phragma, since it is its toughest and really supporting part. The basilar membrane, we recall from the previous chapter, is quite differently attached to the wall at the left and to the wall at the right. At the left it is fastened in a single point; but on the flat wall at the right it is "anchored," so to speak, upwards as well as downwards. We must now answer the question, "What change of form will occur when a leather-like strip is hydraulically, that is, by the pressure of a moving liquid, acted on either from above or from below?"

An *anchored* leather-like strip having the original position of the straight dotted line in Figure 7 must *immediately* assume the position of the solid curve from C to C as soon

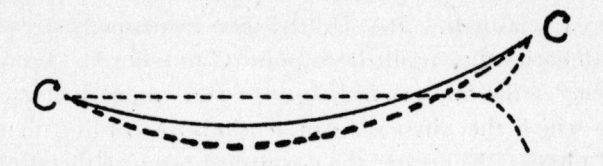

Fig. 7. The straight dotted line, which forks, represents the basilar membrane in its position at rest. The *solid curve* indicates the position *immediately* taken when hydraulic pressure begins to act from above. The dotted curve is one of the catenaries resulting from further pressure.

as hydraulic pressure begins to act on it from above. Incidentally, we recall the fact that the resulting curve has a well established mathematical name. In mechanics it is called a "catenary," i.e., a chain curve. A *chain* hangs in such a curve because there is no tension or only infinitesimal tension from link to link (quite different in a violin string from point to point); but the only force influencing it is the pull of gravity from the outside.

The total *length* of this *solid drawn* catenary is no greater than the sum of the length of the straight line from the left to the point where it forks, plus the length of the upper "anchor chain." *Thus far it is perfectly tensionless.* The dictionary defines "to stretch" as "to draw out to greater length." The change of our leather-like strip into this (first) catenary, therefore, does not involve any stretching, any lengthening, any stressing, any tensioning.

But now suppose that the pressure of the liquid tending

to move downwards increases further. This smoothly curved but yet tensionless cross-section of the basilar membrane now becomes an elastic line first slightly, then increasingly stressed. New catenaries thus result from point C to point C. From a stretching of the first catenary into *further* catenaries, results a force which the physicists call tension. According to the laws of physics, the greater the downward pressure the greater that stretching, that tension, which tends to bring the strip extremely quickly back from a position of a later catenary *to the first* catenary *as soon as* there is any, even the least, *lessening* (though not yet reversal) of the hydraulic force. These later catenaries are not drawn in Figure 7 except one, the dotted one, which symbolizes all of them. But *absolutely* the tension always remains *infinitesimal* and is never comparable to the measurable one of a violin string which makes that string "vibrate." There are *no vibrations* in the phragma.

It is well to have a name for the original position of the phragma (or the basilar membrane) and for the positions resulting from hydraulic pressure. Indeed we shall see later that it is indispensable for the understanding of certain phenomena of hearing to have such names. The Greek word "thesis", which simply means position, is a natural name for the original position. "Parathesis" which means near-by position is a good name for the first catenary. Any one of the later catenaries we name "hyperthesis" as hyper means "beyond" a limit. We shall convince ourselves in our later discussions that, in order to explain what we desire to explain in the phenomena of hearing, it is rarely necessary to distinguish various hypertheses; the name in the singular thus may stand for all of them.

It is a physical law that at the two sides of a border the

force and the counterforce are always of the same quantity, though of opposite algebraical sign. The counterforce exerted by the positions of the later catenaries against the hydraulic pressure may be measured by the distance through which the catenaries more and more recede from the first

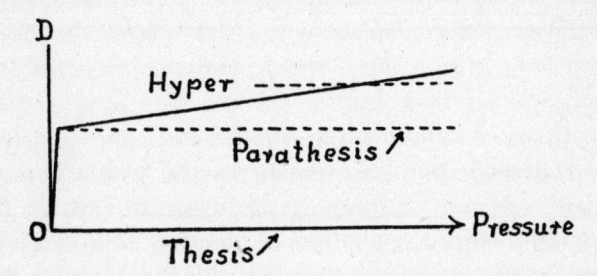

Fig. 8. Minute hydraulic pressure suffices to bring the phragma immediately into one of its paratheses. Further pressure brings it into one of its hypertheses. O-D measures the phragma displacement (in either direction, be it up or down).

catenary. This relation between the variable hydraulic force and the variable recession (displacement) of the basilar membrane can be demonstrated by the mathematical method of using rectangular coordinates in Figure 8.

In order to make Figure 8 small in all directions, both positive and negative hydraulic pressures are measured on the horizontal coordinate from left to right. For one example, if the pressure applied to the phragma is *negative,* the *upward* movement of the phragma is extremely rapid until the upper parathesis is reached. *After* that the rise of the *descriptive curve* (in the figure, two straight lines) of the displacement is very small because *the beginning tension* of the basilar membrane now opposes the growing hydraulic force. If the pressure applied to the phragma is *positive,* the *downward* movement from the thesis is extremely rapid until the lower parathesis is reached. *After* that the slope of the displacement in the figure is very small because *the beginning tension* of the basilar membrane now opposes the hydraulic force. Any measure of the displacement either above the upper parathesis or below the lower parathesis is called a hyperthesis.

We shall later see that the phragma may not only be jerked between the two paratheses; also it may be jerked between any hyperthesis and its adjoining parathesis, there back and forth. Jerks of the latter kind are of immense importance for the efficacy of our sense of hearing in its function of analyzing, as we shall convince ourselves at the proper time.

Now return to Figure 4 and also keep in mind Figure 7. We said in our explanation of the former that Nature had put a limit to the rise or fall of the phragma being displaced. We have in the present chapter given to this limit two distinct names, calling it *parathesis* in its first step, and in the second step (after a slight tension has been produced in *the basilar membrane*) calling the limit *hyperthesis*. In Figure 4 when air pressure on the oval or on the round window has exhausted itself, the point x, or y, must lie the farther away from the windows (and the nearer T), the greater the pressure difference between a minimum and a maximum of the fluctuating air density. Suppose that this pressure difference is so great that when the long bulge (between the windows and x, or y) has lengthened itself even to T, the hydraulic pressure has not yet exhausted itself. All the parts of the more and more lengthened bulge as far as T are now in a hyperthesis. With its ever waxing tension there is then increasing danger that the basilar membrane might burst.

On the boiler of a powerhouse, bursting is prevented up to a high pressure degree, though not absolutely, by a safety valve. Just so here. At T there is a small hole. "Trema" is the Greek word of the anatomists for hole. Through this trema the liquid from the double column of Figure 3 may now be forced without deepening either the upper or the lower hyperthesis any further, that is, without increasing the danger of a burst in the bottom of either the upper or the lower bulge. Thus the bursting is still out of the question although the hydraulic pressure still waxes. The trema at T functions as the safety valve. Nevertheless, like every safety valve it may be abused. A roaring artillery piece may burst the phragma; and then most likely not very far from the windows.

After all these preparatory discussions we are now almost ready to explain the analyzing function of the cochlea. Yet even now a few words must be said first about the manner in which the loudness of an auditory sensation is perceived.

Chapter XI

ON WHAT COCHLEAR CONDITIONS THE PERCEIVED LOUDNESS OF A TONE SENSATION DEPENDS. ALSO FIRST DISCUSSION OF ANALYSIS PERFORMED BY THE COCHLEA

It is reasonable to assume that the greater the number of hair cells which become active as piezo-electric microphones by being jerked, the louder is the tone sensation. Unfortunately it is impossible to count by looking or by instruments the number of hair cells which in a particular case are thus affected. Neither is it possible to reach, any more than remotely, exact theoretical conclusions in this respect by trying to compute what proportionate lengths of the phragma would be jerked up and down by stronger or weaker physical tones. The chief obstacle to computing such proportionate lengths is the fact that the phragma does not possess the same width all along from A to T in Figure 4. It is extremely narrow near A. Away from A it widens at first very rapidly. But a little farther away from A its width increases more and more slowly until, for some length, it becomes about constant. And then, approaching T, it narrows again somewhat. It is a remarkable condition very troublesome for attempting any quantitative theoretical determination of loudness.

Clearly then a minute amount of displaced liquid within

a short distance from A must bring relatively quite a length of the basilar membrane into the first catenary form of its cross-section, into its parathesis. Yet only a little farther away from A, we observe that a many, many times greater amount of liquid can be given room in the same length of "bowl" formed by the catenary of the basilar membrane. Here then a small additional length of the basilar membrane and a very small additional number of hair cells come into operation compared with what happened close to A for an identical amount of liquid taken care of.

There is never any exact proportionality between the number of hair cells in different regions of the phragma functioning and varying physical intensities, that is, energy quantities used up, work done, of a physical tone. Any conclusion offered for a relation between the number of hair cells functioning and a special physical tone intensity must therefore be accepted merely as a guess and estimate having only a remote nearness to actuality. But such computations need not be absolutely rejected. Caution only is needed before accepting them.

For an illustration of tonal analysis we now select the simplest case of a frequency ratio, the ratio 1:2, musically representing the interval called a single octave. Figure 9 shows a wave, technically speaking "one cycle," of the lower tone. Figure 10 shows two cycles of the higher tone. The distance from left to right, from one vertical line to the other, represents the duration of time during which the density changes in the air, the pressure changes occur. We assume now that neither the pressure changes of Figure 9 nor those of Figure 10 occur separately, but that they occur simultaneously and in such a manner that any pressure minimum of Figure 9 occurs exactly at a moment when there is a pressure minimum of Figure 10. When we say this, the acousticians say that we have presumed a definite "phase relation" between the two curves. To find the compound we simply have to pile one curve upon the other; and the result is Figure 11.

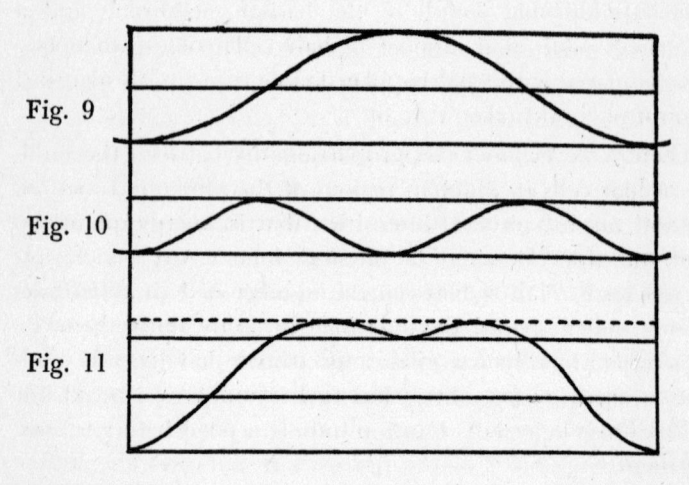

Figs. 9, 10 and 11. A compound air pressure wave. Frequency ratio 1:2.

One of the acoustic problems which has puzzled the scientific world for several centuries is that of understanding how it is possible to hear several tones, lower and higher ones, at the same time. It has been customary to refer to this problem by the question, "How does the ear analyze a sound?" It seems strange that reputable, even famous scientists have thought they have solved this problem by saying that the analysis is brought about "in some way within the brain." That is obviously only a clever (?) way of going around the problem instead of solving it. Neurological science is devoid of all knowledge of brain functions through the consideration of which the problem of sound analysis could be solved. It is not the brain that analyzes a sound; it is the cochlea that does it, and we shall now proceed in showing how.

Now we must refer back to Figure 3. The extent and the velocity of the left-right-left, etc., movement of the *column* of liquid located between A and B depend respectively on the *height* and the *slope* of the air pressure curve. The extent of the length A-x in Figure 4 would be proportional to the *height* of that curve in Figure 11 if the width of the phragma were constant all along. On the other hand the velocity of the end point A of the column of liquid B-A is proportional to the (positive or negative) *slope* of the same pressure curve. Let us first consider exclusively the height in Figure 11 and let us, for simplicity of reasoning, proceed *as if* the width of the phragma were constant all along. As the curve rises, a proportional piece of the phragma is put into the lower parathesis (II in Figure 12) somewhat as shown by the piece from A as far as x in Figure 4. As the curve recedes from its maximum to the next relative minimum, a piece like A-y must pass into the upper parathesis (III in Figure 12) although in the case described by Figure 11 the piece A-y must be shorter than that of Figure 4. Then this same length A-y passes back (IV in Figure 12) into its lower parathesis. Now the curve falls from a great height to a great depth, and a length like A-x is returned (V in Figure 12) to its upper parathesis. For the present we shall neglect the hypertheses altogether.

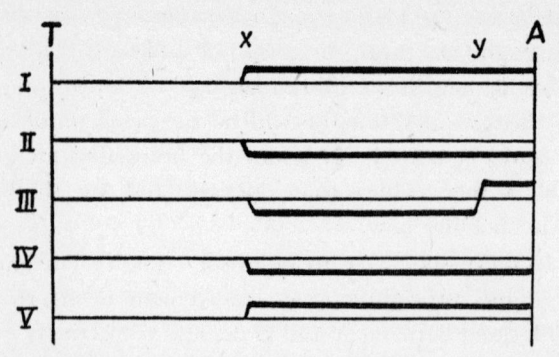

Fig. 12. An example of sound analysis in the cochlea.

As a warning to avoid misunderstandings let us mention here that, of course, we have presumed the happenings of Figure 11 to have occurred *already* during a fraction of a second, so that at the beginning of the wave drawn the piece A-x of Figure 12 is *already* in the upper parathesis and not where it is found, drawn for a different purpose of illustration, at *a* in Figure 4.

In order to demonstrate that thus the sensory analysis of the compound physical sound is brought about in the cochlea, we rely on Figure 12. We look at the length A-y and observe what happens to it *downwards* from I to V in the figure. In the second position, marked II, we see it in the lower parathesis. In the third, marked III, we see it in the upper parathesis. In the fourth, marked IV, we see it in the lower parathesis. In the fifth, marked V, we see it in the upper parathesis. Position V is of course identical with position I, as referred to in the previous paragraph; and now everything is repeated again and again until the physical sound, the air wave or the shaking of the skull, comes to an end.

That during the very short time occupied by the single (compound) pressure wave of Figure 11 this piece A-y of the phragma has been jerked twice is obvious.

Now we look at the length y-x in Figure 12. At II, III and IV we see it steadily in the lower parathesis. In the position marked V, identical with position I, we see it in the upper parathesis. During the time of the pressure wave of Figure 11 the length y-x of Figure 12 has been jerked but once. These jerks repeated in further periods must appear in the perception as a tone sensation of a certain pitch, whichever pitch you wish to imagine; and the jerks of the length A-y must appear as the simultaneous sensation of the higher octave, since the frequency of jerks of the different microphones of the cochlea here is double that of the other microphones, that is, hair cells squeezed. The cochlea has performed the analysis.

One important feature of this cochlear analysis still remains to be pointed out. When we compare Figure 10 with Figure 11, we can not help becoming aware of the fact that the vertical distance between the dotted line and the next solid line in Figure 11 is much smaller than the vertical distance between the maxima and minima in Figure 10. This explains why the length A-y in Figure 12 is so short in comparison with the length y-x. The theoretical conclusion, in the reports of those who have made sensory observations quite generally agreed on, is the *generalization* that lower tones have a power of absorption on the loudness of higher tones. While this has been acknowledged in the scientific literature for nearly a century and was explained by the present writer more than forty years ago, only in more recent years has it become customary to call it "masking;" so we shall adopt this term here.

The masking may be partial, that is, only *reducing* the expected loudness as in the case above, or it may be *complete*, that is, extinguishing the sensation of the higher pitch. In the latter case, if we have a rather weak but easily audible tone of perfectly constant physical intensity, as soon as we add a very strong lower tone the former becomes inaudible and yet, as soon as the lower tone stops, is audible again. We shall here pass over any description in detail (a very complicated task) of all the conditions on which *complete* masking would depend. But we shall immediately show a case in which one might expect complete masking at first, later to see that a completion of the theory shows the masking to be not yet complete.

Chapter XII

MASKING SEEMINGLY OBVIOUS (IN A THEORY TOO SIMPLIFIED) BUT ACTUALLY ABATED BY THE HYPERTHESIS INTERVENING

We return to Figures 9 and 10 with the intention of piling again the latter air pressure curve upon the former. However, we do this only after having made what the acousticians call a "change of phase." We first divide the distance between the two vertical lines into eight equal parts and slide the whole Figure 10 by this amount to the left. Only then do we pile the curve of Figure 10 upon the curve of Figure 9. The result is the curve of Figure 13.

Imagine that Figure 13 is an automobile road on a map and that you are driving on the map in the general direction toward the right. From the mathematical minimum of the curve on the left you are steering your car gently toward your own left shoulder until you meet the "road sign" of a vertical line. Hence you have to steer your car gently toward your right until you meet another road sign. From your experience with Figure 11 you now expect to approach more or less the horizontal line at the bottom of the map. You are disappointed. You have to steer toward your left shoulder and further separate yourself from that bottom line. At the next road sign you change to steering rightwards; and even at the next road sign you continue steering rightwards. Then comes a point where you have to steer leftwards again; and

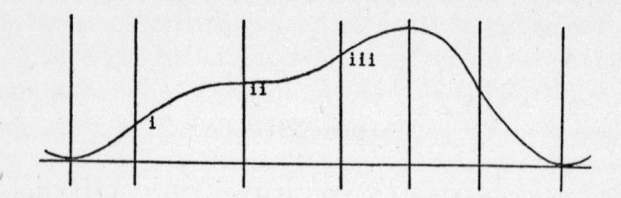

Fig. 13. What a change of phase can bring about. The vertical lines mark the minima and maxima and also the inflection points.

finally you reach the end of your travel, the minimum of the curve.

If you had thought about your driving along the curve of the earlier figure, Figure 11, in a mathematical way, you would have said that from the *minimum at the start* you had to steer leftwards until you met an "inflection point." That is the technical name of mathematicians for such a point where you change steering. You would next pass over a maximum but you made no change there in the direction of steering your car. Then you met another inflection point and a relative minimum; then another inflection point and another maximum. Without changing the steering here you proceeded to another inflection point and there changed your steering; and after that you ended your journey at the minimum on the right of the map of Figure 11. The *important* thing to remember is: that *you never met two immediately successive inflection points*. Between any two inflection points you always met either a (relative) maximum or a (relative) minimum of the curve of Figure 11.

In Figure 13 you discover an entirely different case. You

discover three inflection points (i, ii and iii) which are not in any way separated from one another by either a maximum or a minimum of the curve. Because of the *enormous importance* of this relation of any inflection points, we must give them a distinctive name. We shall call them *grouped inflection points*.

Hitherto we have taken into account only the *extent* of the motion of point A when the liquid column A-B of Figure 3 moves in the directions shown there by the arrows. Now we must fulfill our promise made in the middle of Chapter XI to consider, secondly, also the *velocity* of that point A. If the velocity of point A remained always infinitesimally small, then varying extents of motion would bring varying lengths of the phragma merely into the parathesis and never beyond. But when this velocity is a "finite," a measurable one, the phragma must move into a hyperthesis, more so near A and less so farther away from A. What is the consequence for a case of grouped inflection points?

The *velocity* of A in Figure 3 is determined by the amount of *slope* in a limited region of the curve of air pressure or skull shaking. Jut before the point i in Figure 13 the *slope* of the curve is considerable and whatever phragma piece is below the thesis must have reached a considerable *hyperthesis*. From i to ii the slope, the velocity in question, diminishes until at ii the velocity of the point A has become zero. During that time that phragma piece has a chance to return (although not to the thesis) to the *parathesis* which adjoins this hyperthesis. From the moment ii to the moment iii the slope increases and that phragma piece goes to a *hyperthesis*. Summing up: although the curve has no maximum at ii, that phragma piece has nevertheless been jerked *some-*

what as if there had been a curve maximum at ii followed by a minimum at iii. It has been jerked here between a hyperthesis and its adjoining parathesis (and not between paratheses).

At a first glance in comparing Figure 11 with Figure 13, the higher octave tone sensation to be expected from Figure 12 seemed to be lost in Figure 13. But we have now convinced ourselves that this is not true. Even in Figure 13 the cochlear analysis is thoroughgoing enough to make the higher as well as the lower octave tone audible. The masking of the higher tone is not yet complete.

In order to make the masking complete, to make the higher tone inaudible, the *changes* of slope (not the slope, not the average slope itself) between i and iii would have to be so slight that the distance between that parathesis and that hyperthesis, between which the jerk is expected to occur, would have to be ineffectual. Of course, when the parathesis and the adjunct hyperthesis are so close as to be virtually identical, no jerk between them would occur with such power that it could *charge* some piezo-electric microphones of the cochlea, some hair cells. Naturally that condition can be produced by diminishing the physical intensity of the higher tone more and more relative to the physical intensity of the lower tone. But that condition has not yet been obtained in Figure 13.

It should be added here that the phenomenon of *masking* becomes virtually extinct when the musical *interval* between the two tones is *widened* to more than about two and a half octaves. It is not difficult to explain that; but it is not of sufficient interest in this elementary book to devote the rather large space needed for extending the explanation of masking to cover that mainly negative fact.

To those who are interested in music, the incomplete kind of masking which consists in *this reduction* of (the *higher* tone's) loudness, although in a lesser degree than might be expected, is more important than any other. Yet one must *not* conclude that the perception of a *low pitch* could in no manner be interfered with by the presence of *higher* tones or noises, especially noises. First, the psychological function of *attention* to the lower pitch might easily suffer. Masking by a withdrawal of attention would require a neurological explanation and would not fall within the sphere of cochlear functioning. Second, the mere cochlear mechanism as we understand it in this book can reduce the loudness of the lowest simultaneous tone if the higher tones or noises are of such physical intensity that the *whole* length of the phragma becomes involved. We have seen that the lowest pitch must result from jerks of the phragma nearer the trema than the jerks giving the perception of the higher pitches expected under the circumstances. When jerks, which are to serve the lowest pitch, are thrown to a greater or lesser extent into the very trema, such parts of them would *functionally* not exist, since the phragma and its sensitive cells have ceased to exist there. The loudness of the lowest tone would then be reduced beyond our expectation. Thus there would be true *cochlear* masking of the lowest tone because of the excessive physical intensity of simultaneously produced higher tones or noises.

Chapter XIII

TWO KINDS OF BEATS: UNISON BEATS AND MULTIPLE FREQUENCY BEATS

This chapter will be divided into two parts which will be marked (A) and (B).

(A) Sometimes one hears a tone "beating," fluctuating in loudness with great regularity, perhaps only about once per second, perhaps as many as twenty or more times per second. *One kind* of beats has been known for centuries and always been easily understood. But a *second kind, although known for a hundred years* in the literature of acoustics (see Stumpf's *Tonpsychologie* II, 463-464, 492-497), has more recently been taken for something which it is not and will be discussed *separately* under (B). The former kind results from the simultaneous existence of physical vibrations which differ very slightly in frequency, so slightly that they are not musically distinguished in pitch but called "unison." Whenever one series of air pressure waves is accompanied by another series from a source which is quite independent of the source of the former, and the frequency is not exactly the same, a maximum of the one air pressure curve can not remain forever coexisting with a maximum of the other air pressure curve. Gradually the one series of waves will slide over the other series. After a brief time a minimum of one curve will coincide with a maximum of the other. At that moment, if the intensities of the two tones are alike, the two waves will cancel each other and the actual wave height will be zero. Soon the two wave series will reach double height when one maximum piles up over another maximum. Naturally there will be fluctuations in the auditory sensation, too, in loudness, from nothing to great loudness, to nothing again, and so forth.

If the intensities of the physical tones are not alike, then there will be great loudness followed by a reduction of loudness to something less, though not to zero, followed by a greater loudness and so forth. All this is so self-evident that we need not try to explain it further; nor do we have to illustrate it by a figure.

Nevertheless, there is a deceptive kind of *unison beats* which is occasionally in the scientific literature confused with the kind of beats which will be discussed later under (B) in the second half of the present chapter. It is simply a case of unison beats in disguise. In this case a lower tone is accompanied by a physical "overtone." What is an overtone? Vibrating and musically used bodies, of which a stretched violin string is an excellent example, very often, even usually, vibrate not only as a whole length but also as fractions, $\frac{1}{2}$, $\frac{1}{3}$, $\frac{1}{4}$, $\frac{1}{5}$, etc., of the whole length. The violinist is familiar with the fact, for he may kill the "fundamental" tone belonging to the whole length by touching the vibrating string very gently, barely, with a finger tip in one of the fractional division points. Thus the fundamental is made impossible, but certain "overtones" of the string are still possible and audible. Now in any case like that, for example, where the tone 100 is accompanied by, say, the *overtone* 400, and where then a physically independent tone is added, say, 402, two beats per second naturally result. These beats are nothing new. They are simply an example of the first kind of beats we have mentioned and have already disposed of theoretically, unison beats. They have nothing to do with the second kind we are to discuss now; and hereafter we presuppose two "pure" tones, "pure fundamentals" *without any overtones.*

(B) A comparison of Figures 11 and 13 leads to the theoretical explanation of the *second kind of beats.* One frequency here is a *multiple* of the other. There is no unison. Suppose we obtain a further illustrative figure by piling the air pressure curve of Figure 10 upon the curve of Figure 9 only after shifting Figure 10 twice as much to the left as we did in order to obtain Figure 13. We do not draw here this third compound curve because it would have all the features of Figure 11 with only an irrelevant difference: it would be Figure 11 turned upside down.

Now we shift Figure 10 again, and now three times the distance to the left which we used to obtain Figure 13; and we pile again the one curve upon the other. The result would be a fourth compound curve which would have all the features of Figure 13 with only the irrelevant difference of being Figure 13 turned upside down. Thus we have *a total of four compound curves.* We can save space by omitting the printing of the two curves which are merely two others placed upside down.

We have already seen that, if it were not for the *hyperthesis* which "resuscitates" it, the higher tone in Figure 13 would be *completely* masked. Nobody, therefore, will contradict us if we assert that under the conditions of either Figure 11 or its "upside down" the higher tone would be to the hearer noticeably *louder* than under the conditions of either Figure

13 or its "upside down." We can make the same assertion in other words as follows and state a very important general fact: When two tones of *multiple frequency* are heard simultaneously, the higher tone to the hearer is *louder whenever a minimum of one curve coincides with a maximum* of the other curve, *less loud* when a minimum of one curve *never coincides* with a maximum of the other curve.

Now take as an example the case of a lower (but strictly "pure") tone of the frequency of 200 cycles. Add to it from an independent source a tone of the frequency 401. This, thus is what musicians would call a slightly mistuned octave interval, i.e., ratio 1:2. Think of a horse and an ass running a race. Ordinarily the ass would make 400 "steps" while the horse is making 200 "steps." But the "jockey" of the ass has been loaded with a few pounds of lead, and the steps of the ass have been shortened in the proportion in which 400 is less than 401. The ass on the track is seen to slide slowly backwards in comparison with where at any moment we see the horse. That is what happens to the curves of Figures 9 and 10. Curve 9 (the "horse") gains over curve 10 (the "ass") and slides forward over the latter until after exactly one second the maximum of curve 9 stands again over a minimum of curve 10.

During this relative sliding the compound curve changes from Figure 11 to Figure 13 to Figure 11 placed upside down to Figure 13 placed upside down and ends in a compound which is a repetition of Figure 11. In accordance with the second paragraph back there must be fluctuations in loudness, alias "beats;" and two beats per second when the tone 400 is mistuned by changing its frequency of cycles from 400 to 401. *The greater loudness* occurs with Figure 11 and Figure 11 upside down than with Figure 13 and Figure 13 upside down.

An overcritical reader at this point might heckle us: "You just derived from the theory the conclusion that you hear the pitch 400 beating twice per second. But *ought we not* to hear only *one* beat per second when 400 is mistuned only into 401?"

What is the heckler's logic? Does he insist that a correct conclusion from the theory of *unison beats* must be identical with a correct conclusion from the theory of *multiple frequency beats?* The present writer does not, indeed can not, scold the heckler. In a previous publication, in a magazine, the present writer, too, succumbed to the heckler's false logic. Nevertheless the logic is false because the two kinds of beats have an entirely different origin. In the case of unison beats we have nothing but an instance of the general physical phenomenon of interference in wave mechanics. The cochlea and its anatomy and functioning have no responsibility for the fact of physical interference. In optics, also, we know of physical interference. In radio waves, also, the engineers know physical interference. Plain *physical* interference has been disposed of under (A) in the first half of this chapter. Nothing has ever been described by *physicists* which is analogous to the beats (B) caused by *combining a unit frequency with a mistuned integer-multiple frequency in the cochlea.*

In one respect the heckler's challenge is quite welcome. Theories ought always to be tested by experiment. When Galileo had *thought out* his law of falling bodies, he made some experiments to test it. He threw some objects from the famous tower of Pisa. He let some objects slide down inclined planes. His experimental results agreed broadly with his "law" although they were far too inaccurate to permit him to *derive* the law logically from his few experiments. Since then far more accurate experiments have verified Galileo's law. Experiments to test very accurately our theoretical conclusions concerning the second class (B) of beats should be very welcome. Nobody has made them yet. The present writer regrets that the extremely expensive instruments for such an experiment are not available to him. Everybody has agreed for a hundred years that these beats are audible; but nobody has ever raised the question (outside of the present book) *what the exact rate per second is* of mistuned multiple frequency beats. Let us hope that somebody who is fortunate enough to be able to obtain all the necessary instrumental equipment will make the experiments and test the theory.

Above we have used the octave, ratio 1:2, for our theoretical reasoning simply because thus there was no need for drawing figures in addition to those which we had already. The same kind of beats, that is, mistuned multiple frequency beats, is heard, however, and the explanation is the same, when the ratio of the two tones is 1:3, 1:4, 1:5, 1:6, etc. We can make the following generalized statement. Let us call n the cycle frequency of the lower tone and m the cycle frequency of the higher tone under condition that m is an integer-multiple of n. Now we mistune m by a very slight additional or subtractional quantity which we call x. Or we mistune n by the quantity xn/m. In either case we can count, according to the theory of the cochlea, $2x$ beats of the higher tone per second.

Our statement that the multiple frequency beats have been taken for something which they are not, calls for an elaboration. They have been taken for unison beats of an (auxiliary and) mistuned physical tone, the above m, not with a physical overtone of n, excluded in the experiment, but *with a ghostlike* "subjective (aural) harmonic" or *subjective overtone* of n, the lower physical tone, which some authors assert "is heard but is inaudible." This nonsense has been derived from several utterly impossible hypotheses of which the chief one is the assertion of true "vibrations" in the phragma within so-called "resonating zones." Since there is no permanent tension in the phragma, there can be no such "vibrations" there. It is justified therefore to regard these "subjective (aural) harmonics" which nobody has heard but which are dragged in to explain the multiple frequency beats, as mere "ghosts."

As a matter of sensory fact, the definition of *multiple frequency beats* given above requires an amplification. The same (by origin) kind of beats are heard when two frequencies are *both multiples* of a non-existing but only mathematically imagined *unit frequency*. For example, if ("unit" frequency 100 not existing) the frequencies to be mistuned are 600 and 700, beats can be made audible. The number per second simply depends on how many times the phase relation is restored. If 700 is mistuned into 701, the original phase relation is restored six times, and two beats are to be expected for each restoration of the phase relation "a minimum coinciding with a maximum," or, more popularly speaking, "a valley coinciding with a crest."

Algebraically we should say: If the higher frequency m is mistuned by x cycles, we hear $2xn/(m-n)$ beats per second. If the lower frequency n is mistuned by x cycles, we hear $2xm/(m-n)$ beats per second. In the above example $m-n$

equals 100; $(m-n)$ is the non-existing unit frequency.

In the acoustical literature such beats are sometimes spoken of as beats of mistuned consonances. That is objectionable because consonance is no term belonging in *physics*. We shall see in Chapter XXII that the term "consonance" is an obsolete *musical* term no longer influencing modern composers. The scientifically correct usage is simply to state that any small-term ratios differing by unit, such as 4:5, 7:8, 10:11, etc., etc., also exhibit beats when slightly mistuned,— and without the need of those imaginary "subjective (aural) harmonics."

Chapter XIV

THE TONES OF TARTINI

In the year 1745 a German musical writer, Sorge, in a book on musical composition reported the curious fact that, when he produced two physical tones together, usually on the organ, he could hear one or more additional, but still lower (never higher), tones which he did not expect. In 1753 the French physicist, Romieu, reported the same fact. In 1754 the Italian violinist and writer on musical theory, Tartini, reported the same fact of lower tones being audible contrary to all expectations. Because among those who independently made this discovery, Tartini was most widely known in the musical world of Europe, these tones were soon customarily referred to as the tones of Tartini. And by this name we call them here.

In the acoustical literature the facts about the tones of Tartini have been most extraordinarily distorted, in many books of various authors. Especially regrettable is the accusation, thrown against Tartini, of having reported the pitches of these tones wrongly in musical notation, of having committed octave errors in writing them down. His accusers deceived themselves; *they* committed the errors. The accusation is ridiculous in the case of a man of Tartini's musical accomplishments. We now select a particular instance of the tones of Tartini for theoretical explanation.

The dotted curves of Figure 14 represent two primary tones

from totally independent sources. It is important to emphasize the mutual independence of their origin. We shall mention later a great confusion which has resulted from a lack of

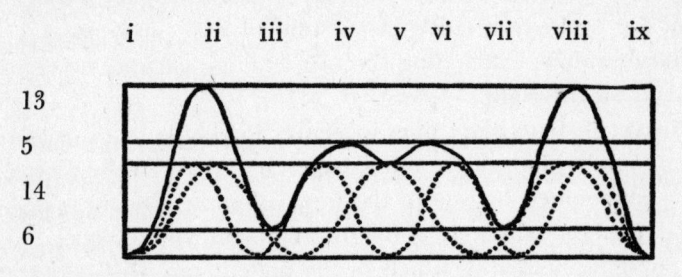

      i   ii   iii   iv   v vi vii   viii   ix

13
5
14
6

Fig. 14. A compound air wave. Frequency ratio 3:4.

distinction between *mutually independent sources* and a *single source* issuing simultaneously two primary tones. The frequency ratio here is 3:4. The phase between the physical tone 3 and the physical tone 4 has been chosen by the draftsman arbitrarily so that he found the drawing of the figure most convenient. The phase is of little importance in our present discussion of the tones of Tartini. When one of the primary curves is piled upon the other, the resulting compound is drawn in a continuous line. The five horizontal lines drawn in Figure 14 are for the purpose of estimating the approximate vertical distances between the pressure maxima and the pressure minima of the compound curve. After dividing the distance from the bottom line to the top line into 38 parts, the lowest distance amounts to about six of these thirty-eighths, the next above to about fourteen, the next to five, and the top one to about thirteen of the thirty-eighths.

In Figure 15 we see nine auxiliary horizontal lines. In regard to time, the top one belongs to the minimum with which the compound curve starts on the left in Figure 14. The one next below belongs to the following maximum in Figure 14. We need nine of these auxiliary lines in Figure 15 because the compound curve has a total of nine maxima and minima combined including the two extreme minima on the left and on the right.

The vertical auxiliary lines in Figure 15 enable us to speak of four subdivisions of the phragma, each of these subdivisions being represented by one of the four columns, plus an additional column which is going to represent that length of the phragma toward T which in the present case will be left

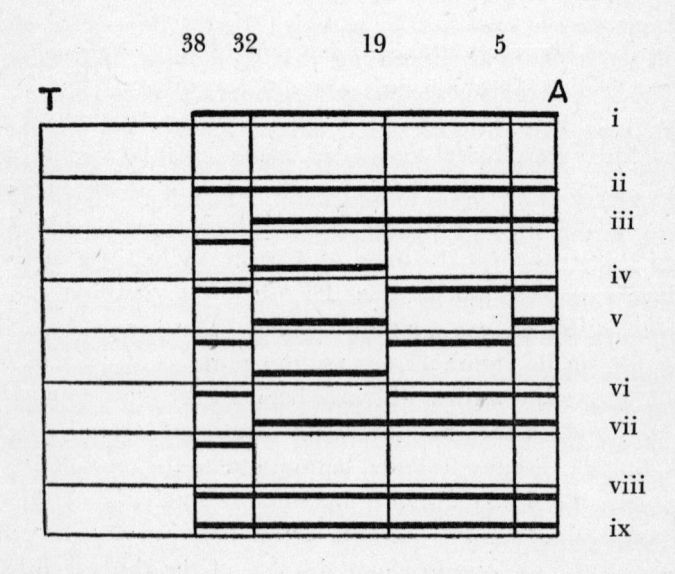

Fig. 15. Illustration of the analysis of the compound 3:4 by the cochlea.

functionless. The width of these columns could be used as an indicator of the relative loudness of each pitch sensation, were it not for the fact that the cochlea near the windows carries an extremely narrow phragma, which further quickly widens and later widens very slowly, even narrows again near T. In our drawings we can not ever indicate how long the functioning part of the phragma is in comparison with the functionless one nearer T. Any conclusion drawn from the relative width of those columns in Figure 15 and similar figures must be regarded as very conditional and preliminary. *Especially* the column on the right deceives us by its apparent narrowness.

If we desire to get a picture which is very simple, very clear and very easy to examine, let us forget for the time being all about the hyperthesis and assume that both above and below the thesis the phragma cannot pass beyond the parathesis.

We now have to look alternately at Figure 14 and at Figure 15. Starting at the left in the former, the pressure rises quickly to an absolute maximum. Therefore Figure 15 begins on top with a large length of the phragma, measured as 38 units, first being in the upper parathesis and next, directly below, appearing as having now been jerked to a position in the lower parathesis. We assume, naturally, that all that is described in the total figure has already been going on for some time, at least a considerable fraction of a second, so that we do not have to begin our explanatory figure with the phragma at lasting rest in the thesis. We begin with a long piece of the phragma in the upper parathesis, as has just been stated.

The pressure now falls, without, however, reaching at once the absolute minimum of the curve, since the fall amounts only to 13 plus 5 plus 14 units, that is, 32 units. Nevertheless, the pressure drop is great; and we see in Figure 15 that 32 of the 38 units of length have been jerked to the upper parathesis. The remainder, nearer T, from point 32 to point 38, remains virtually in the lower parathesis because no displaced liquid reaches this length of six units to get it away from the position which it occupies at the moment; at least not within a time that would make any difference, have any consequence here, although we feel sure that in so long a time as a few seconds it would undoubtedly resume its place in the thesis.

The pressure now rises a little less than it last dropped, and 19 unit lengths of the phragma are jerked into the lower parathesis. But beyond and nearer T there remains for the time being a piece of the phragma in the upper parathesis, and still farther a piece in the lower parathesis.

The pressure now drops, though not very greatly; and 5 length units near A are jerked into the upper parathesis. All three pieces nearer T remain where they were last, as Figure 15 shows at v. The pressure then rises 5 units; and the same short length near A is jerked back into the lower parathesis, for which see vi in Figure 15. Now 19 units are jerked upwards. Then 32 units are jerked downwards. The large pressure drop at the end of the period, from viii to ix, brings all the 38 length units of the phragma into the upper parathesis, the position of the whole phragma now being the very one with which we started on top of Figure 15.

Now we have to look at each of the four columns, scrutinizing them from top to bottom and counting the jerks. The phragma length nearest A is jerked four times during the period. The next phragma length goes down, then up, down-

down-down staying without change, and then up, then down and up for a third time.

All the hair cells, the piezo-electric microphones of the cochlea, which are located within the former phragma length receive 4 electron charges during the period. We get the pitch sensation of the "tone 4." All the hair cells, the little microphones, which are located in the latter phragma length receive 3 electron charges during the period. We get the pitch sensation of the "tone 3." The *analysis* has been performed by the cochlea. But the cochlea does more than that. It also *adds* the tones of Tartini.

When we count the jerks within the column between the points 19 and 32, we observe the following. This phragma length goes down; then it gets up and remains up, up, up, up. Then it gets down and up. Here now we are confronted with a problem which can not be solved by any arm chair philosopher. There is a dilemma, so-called. Can the theory sit on one of the horns? Or can it sit on the other horn? Or is there a way of sitting on both horns?

First, it is true that we count two jerks within the period. Second, the jerks do not succeed one another in very exact intervals of time; there is a jerk, then a long time interval, then a jerk, then a shorter interval of time, then a jerk and so forth. But what does the brain "say to this" charging of the microphones? Do we have the sensation of the pitch 2? Or does the brain accept the electric charges separated by the short interval at ix (or i, which is the same) as if it were only a single charge followed by nothing from iv to vii? No neurological experiment has ever been performed with the intention of answering these questions. No neurological facts are known from which an answer could be derived by logic. It is even thinkable that the brain would accept some of these microphonic charges as meaning the pitch of the "tone 1" and at the same time would accept some of them as meaning the pitch of the "tone 2," thus "sitting on both horns of the dilemma." Only neurologists by properly devised experiments can solve this problem.

The last column, between the points 32 and 38, unequivocally gives us one jerk per period and accordingly the "tone 1" as the tone of Tartini. Whether a Tartini tone "2" is *also* audible here, is not only theoretically *uncertain;* careful observers, listening, have *not* yet been able to *agree* whether this pitch is simultaneously present or not. For musical-psychological reasons it is often rather difficult to tell with assurance whether a higher octave tone (2) accompanies the lower tone (1). This difficulty of judging has nothing to do with "masking." It results from the musical-psychological fact of the great melodious affinity (compare Chapter XIX) of octave tones, the lower drawing the attention and monopolizing it. It is a matter of psychological judgment trying to avoid a possible illusion.

Chapter XV

ASSERTED BY SOME AUTHORS, BUT NON-EXISTING TONES OF TARTINI

In the nineteenth century certain authors of books on tones and music became struck with the idea that the tones of Tartini should have some causal relation to arithmetical differences which, they thought, one could figure out directly and indirectly from the ratio terms of the primary tones, and which should be accepted as a "causal explanation." For example, in the case of 3 and 4 discussed in the preceding chapter they would say that the tone 1 was the difference between 3 and 4, and that by further subtracting 1 from 3 one got the difference 2. "Quod erat demonstrandum," i. e., "this is the proof," they exclaimed like the ancient Greek geometrician, Euclid, at the end of a demonstration. As a matter of truth nothing whatsoever was proved and scientifically explained by such *subtracting*.

In the case of the combination of the primary tones 3 and 5, issuing from certified independent sources, which we shall discuss further in the next chapter, the same writers argued that the Tartini tone 2 must be audible because 2 is the arithmetical difference between 3 and 5, and that the tone 1 must be audible because one can subtract 2 from 3. One thus gets 1; and 4 must be audible, they said, because it is the difference of 5 and 1. As a matter of fact, by the testimony of listening witnesses, the tone 1 is the only one which one can be sure of, whereas it is highly dubious whether the tone 2 is audible at all, in spite of arithmetic telling us that 5 minus 3 produces 2. As to 4, there are no witnesses willing to testify.

Take as another example the primary tones 4 and 9. Now follow the advice of those writers and subtract 4 from 9. You get 5. Neither Tartini nor any other witness has yet sworn to have heard 5. But when you now subtract 4 from the *inaudible* 5, the result is 1. This tone 1 is the *only* Tartini tone for the ratio 4:9 of which careful listeners are sure. The principles of Science demand that every combination of primary tones ought to be investigated by a theoretical discussion of what occurs in the cochlea and by a succeeding verification of the theory or a denial by unprejudiced experimental listening. Very little is to be found in the acoustic literature about such a combination of individual *theoretical* cases with individual *experimentation* on the same cases by actual listening of musical observers. Our literature abounds with dogmatic assertions and unprincipled generalizations.

That arithmetical differences, direct or indirect, between the ratio terms of the primary tones play a sort of limited role in the tones of Tartini is undeniable. Therefore it has been rather customary during the last hundred years to call the Tartini tones "difference tones." From what has been said in the preceding paragraphs it follows that the choice of such a terminology is not a fortunate one. Therefore this book has preferred to call them simply in honor of one of their early discoverers by his name; thus we do not obligate ourselves to logical conclusions from uncertain premises. And the book will continue to call them Tartini tones, and will continue to describe them as resulting from the hydraulic-mechanical functioning of the cochlea, not as resulting from arithmetic.

Some of those writers on physiological acoustics who were enamored of the idea that the mere arithmetical concept of "difference" was acceptable as a scientific explanation now fell into another error of scientific logic. Mathematicians treat differences and sums as two members of the same family of concepts. So some writers concluded that, if there were difference tones, there *should* also be summation tones. They were groundlessly encouraged in this conclusion by the interesting event that the distinguished German physicist, Helmholtz, (1821-1894) discovered a remarkable physical fact to which the term "summation tones" was quite properly applied. Such *physical* summation tones (and like-wise difference tones, together called by Helmholtz "combination tones") come into existence when air is permitted to escape simultaneously through "two gates" from a single air room where it is kept at more than atmospheric pressure, say, from an organ bellows. Two examples are expressly mentioned by Helmholtz: a harmonium where the air escapes through *two* reeds and a rotating siren where the air escapes through *two* concentric circles of holes. No listener need be employed to prove the existence of such summation tones, since any suitable recording instrument supplied with proper resonators can write their waves on a sheet of paper as it can write any other physical wave on a sheet of paper for the eye to look at. Even a totally deaf person who is not blind can see such summation waves on the paper. No cochlea function comes into play for that effect.

But the question of Tartini tones produced as auditory sensations *by the cochlea* is a totally different question.

Neither Tartini nor any other musician nor any other reliable listener has ever been able to report that he heard "summation tones" when two moderately loud primary tones of certified *independent sources* were brought to play upon the cochlea. Nobody has ever heard the Tartini tone 7 when the primary tones were 3 and 4. Nobody has ever heard the Tartini tone 8 when the primary tones were 3 and 5. Nobody has ever heard the Tartini tone 12 when the primary tones were 5 and 7. Nobody has ever heard the Tartini tone 13 when the primary tones were 4 and 9. The cochlea produces no sensation of summation tone pitches.

Chapter XVI

ANOTHER EXAMPLE OF A TARTINI TONE

The curve of Figure 16 represents the compound curve which results from combining two primary tones from two totally independent sources which act on the cochlea windows or shake the skull. The frequency ratio is 3:5. The physical intensities have been chosen so that the independent air pressure curves have equal amplitudes. This does not mean that the physical *energy* of the two tones is the same. The

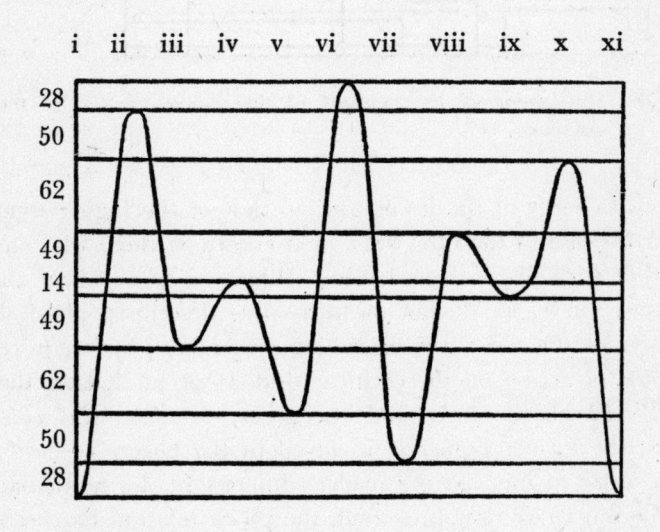

Fig. 16. A compound air wave. Frequency ratio 3:5.

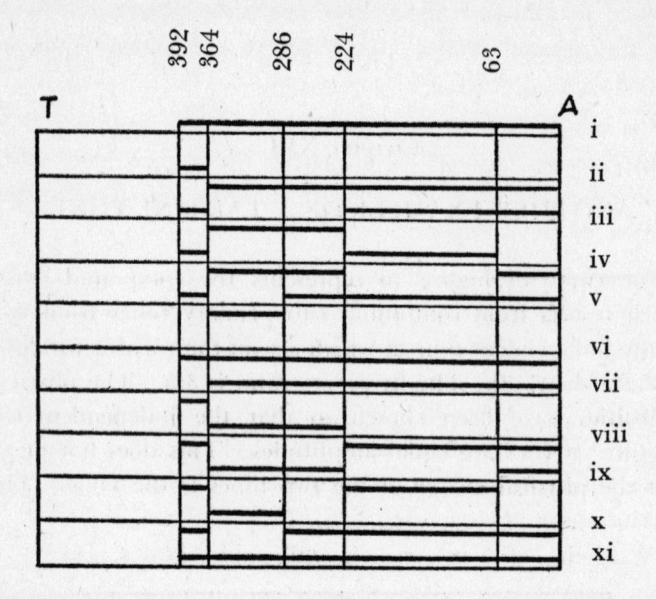

Fig. 17. Illustration of the analysis of the compound 3:5 by the cochlea.

physical energy of the lower tone to that of the higher tone is in this case in the ratio 9:25, as is known to those who are familiar with physical mechanics. When we speak of an air *pressure* curve, we do not mean a curve describing physical energy; we mean a curve describing a *variable physical force* capable of acting on the cochlea windows or of shaking the skull. In physics force and energy are not identical concepts; the former is merely involved in the latter.

In order to increase the reader's interest in the particular compound curve now presented, the phase relation has been chosen arbitrarily as a rather odd one, defined in the next chapter for those readers who might be interested in it. For the general reader knowledge of the phase is of no concern.

The ten horizontal lines in Figure 16 are auxiliary lines drawn for the purpose of estimating the approximate vertical distances between the pressure maxima and the pressure minima of the compound curve.

In Figure 17 we see eleven auxiliary horizontal lines. The top one in regard to time belongs to the minimum with which the compound curve starts in Figure 16 on the left. The auxiliary line next below belongs to the first following maximum in Figure 16. We need eleven of these auxiliary lines in Figure 17 because the compound curve has a total of eleven maxima and minima combined including the two extreme minima on the left and on the right.

The vertical auxiliary lines in Figure 17 enable us to speak of five subdivisions of the phragma, each of these subdivisions being represented by one of the five columns, plus an additional column which is going to represent that length of the phragma toward T which in the present case will be left functionless. The width of these columns could be used as an indicator of the relative loudness of each pitch sensation were it not for the fact that the cochlea near the windows has an extremely narrow phragma, which at first widens quickly and later very slowly, even narrows again near T. In our drawings we cannot ever indicate how long the functioning part of the phragma is in comparison with the functionless part nearer T. Any conclusion drawn from the relative width of these columns with respect to relative loudness must be regarded as very conditional and preliminary.

Especially the column on the right at A deceives by its apparent narrowness.

If we desire to get a picture which is very simple, very clear and very easy to examine, we forget for the time being all about the hyperthesis and assume that both above and below the thesis the phragma can not pass beyond the parathesis (although that is not the real condition).

We now have to look alternately at Figure 16 and at Figure 17. Starting at the left in the former, the pressure rises rapidly to a relative maximum. Therefore Figure 17 begins on top with a large length of the phragma, measured in 392 units, first being in the upper parathesis; it is followed at ii by a large length of 364 units in the lower parathesis. Those readers who happen to be interested in computing these numerical values will find some hints in the next chapter. We assume naturally that all this has already been going on for a considerable fraction of a second, so that we do not have to begin our explanation with the phragma at rest in the thesis. We begin exactly as Figure 17 ends below at xi, since the end of the compound pressure curve is also again its beginning.

The pressure now falls, without, however, reaching the absolute minimum of the curve, since the fall is only of 50+62+49+14+49, that is, of 224 units. Nevertheless the pressure drop is great; and we see in Figure 17, at iii, 224 unit lengths raised to the upper parathesis. All those farther toward T remain where they were at ii, or virtually so, since no outside pressure change has influenced them.

From iii to iv in Figure 16 the pressure force rises 63 units; and in Figure 17 at iv 63 phragma lengths have been put into the lower parathesis. All the units farther away from the windows are left in the very positions in which they were at iii.

From iv to v in Figure 16 there is a pressure drop of 125 units. In Figure 17 at v the first 63 have come up; the next 161 were up already and thus did not have to be moved up; that leaves 62 farther ones to be moved up. The result is that we find a total of 286 in the upper parathesis. Those units which lie farther toward T remain where they were located at iv.

From v to vi in Figure 16 the pressure rises 314 units. Those phragma pieces lying between point 286 and point 364 are already down. They amount to 78 units. Thus all the 392 are now in the lower parathesis, at vi.

From vi to vii in Figure 16 there is a pressure drop of 364 units. In Figure 17 at vii we find 364 length units in the upper parathesis. The remaining 28 which are in function are left where they were at vi, that is, in the lower parathesis.

From vii to viii in Figure 16 there is a pressure rise of 224 units. In Figure 17 at viii we find the first 224 length units having been jerked from the upper into the lower parathesis. Those still farther away from the windows remain where they were at vii.

From viii to ix in Figure 16 the pressure falls 63 units. Accordingly in Figure 17 at ix we find the first 63 length units in the upper parathesis. All the other length units of the phragma remain where they were at viii.

From ix to x the pressure rises 125 units. What happens here is just the reverse of what happened between iv and v. Thus we find at x in Figure 17 a total of 286 in the lower parathesis. Those units which lie farther toward T remain where they were located at ix.

From x to xi in Figure 16 the pressure falls 314 units. The units which were down at x amount to 286 plus 28, or a total of 314. Accordingly all the 392 functioning length units are now in the upper parathesis. That is, we find everything exactly as it was at our start at i.

Now we have to count the number of jerks received by the hair cells during the period. For that purpose we have to look from above down each column in Figure 17.

In the first column, near A, we easily count five jerks. In the second column we find this: from up a motion down, then up-up-up completing the first jerk; then down and up making the second jerk; then down-down-down and up for the third jerk. In the next column we find up, down-down-down and up for the first jerk; then down and up-up-up for the second jerk; then down and up for the third jerk. Thus the microphones of the cochlea which belong to the first column receive 5 electron charges per period and we have the pitch sensation 5. The microphones of the cochlea which belong to the second and third columns from the right of Figure 17 receive 3 electron charges per period and give us the pitch sensation 3. Thus the cochlea has *analyzed* the compound in accordance with our expectations.

But the cochlea does *more than analyze*. In the fourth column from the right of Figure 17 we find: up, then down-down-down-down-down and up completing one jerk; this is followed by four further ups, so that the microphones do not receive more than a single charge during the period. In the fifth column we find up-up-up-up-up followed by down-down-down-down-down and the final up, so that the microphones of this column likewise receive only a single charge during the period. Thus these two columns explain the existence of the Tartini tone 1. In addition to analyzing, the cochlea *creates*.

In the literature of physiological acoustics are found dogmatic notions that the Tartini tones 2 and 4 should also be audible. From the theoretical analysis of the compound curve of Figure 16 this is not to be expected. Let us hope that reliable observers of trained musical attentiveness will devote themselves to the task of answering this and many analogous questions *experimentally by listening*. If the Tartini tone 1 is the only additional tone heard when the primary tones are 3 and 5, this is a striking argument against referring to the Tartini tones as "difference tones," which is often done in the acoustical literature, for plain arithmetic tells us that 1 is not the difference between 3 and 5. The term "difference tones" is not based on sound scientific theory but on imaginative speculation, which sometimes even sees an identity between beats and Tartini tones and calls the latter "misinterpreted beats," as if the sensations named the tones of Tartini were auditory "illusions" analogous to geometric-optical "illusions." There is nothing illusory to the factual existence of the tones of Tartini.

Chapter XVII

COMPUTATION OF ORDINATE DIFFERENCES

This chapter should be left unread by those who are uninterested in or unfamiliar with elementary trigonometry, since all the other chapters of the book are entirely comprehensible without it.

In order to draw definite conclusions from such compound pressure curves as Figures 11, 13, 14 and 16, the ordinate values of the curves ought to be computed with the aid of trigonometric tables. All the maxima and minima of Figure 16 have been computed with special care. The phase relation in this figure is indicated in the following equation, so that any one interested in recomputing and testing the quoted values can do so without hesitation or difficulty.

$$y = \sin 3(x+30) + \sin 5(x+12)$$

Acousticians who compute, or graphically with approximation construct, compounds of sinusoidal curves, commonly draw the curves in such a manner that the line passing through the inflection points of the sinusoids is used as the abscissa axis. That is natural for those who desire to discuss *vibrations*. But, as we have convinced ourselves, there are no vibrations in the cochlea. There are only *phragma jerks*. In order to derive conclusions it is therefore necessary to draw our curves so that the *absolute minima* lie on the base line. Then only can we readily construct such derivative

Figures as 12, 15 and 17. The former method of drawing compound curves has long served the sinister result of retarding the understanding of the real functioning of the cochlea, has helped to strengthen and preserve the absurd belief in tuned and resonating (string-like) phragma zones. Such "tuning" would be a physical possibility only if the phragma were crosswise under permanent (i.e., static) tension as the strings of a violin are when the violinist is ready to play. Such static tension is biologically impossible. In addition to this fundamental impossibility, in recent years anatomical dissection of the living cochlea in animals has demonstrated to the eye that there is no tension whatsoever in the phragma while it is at rest, non-functioning. Figure 7 has shown us how *tension temporarily develops* during functioning only *after* the phragma has passed into the first catenary and is then driven into a further catenary, the hyperthesis; and after the function the tension is gone again.

The phase relation of Figure 16 is a rather odd one compared with phase relations which are usually chosen for illustration. This odd phase relation has been selected for the very reason that a critic may not argue against theoretical conclusions on the basis of saying that what may be true for the more customary phase relations might come to be untrue for a more odd phase relation. Well, that is the reason why the odd one is presented here.

The present writer has also computed the ordinates in those phase relations which in printed publications are more usual. The theoretical conclusions with respect to the tones of Tartini remain virtually the same in all these cases.

There are certain books on physiological acoustics the authors of which *felt the truth* of what was said above concerning the impossibility of permanent tension in the cochlea, and accordingly the impossibility of tuned resonators being ready in the cochlea to "vibrate." Unfortunately they dared not declare their disbelief; they thought that they nevertheless *had to believe* in such resonators in the cochlea because otherwise, they said, one would have to assume that tonal analysis was "in some mysterious way performed in the brain." This latter, utterly unreasonable "escape" from a bad thought could easily have been avoided by those authors if they had not willingly abstained from thinking out the analyzing function of the cochlea in the way in which it has been presented in the first sixteen chapters of this book.

Chapter XVIII

SUMMARY OF THE FUNCTION OF THE COCHLEA. DEAFNESS

The cochlea makes it possible for us to hear several tones at the same moment, or if we prefer to say it in other words, to be conscious of several pitch sensations at the same time. If any one wishes to state the same fact in the words that "the cochlea is a tonal analyzer" the latter statement is also acceptable. But if any one should interpret the statement as meaning that in a physical *mixture of very many* sinusoidal air pressure variations *all of them* would simultaneously become pitch sensations in consciousness, such an interpretation of "tonal analysis" would be far from the truth. Nevertheless this latter interpretation of "tonal analysis" was actually proposed by the German physicist, Ohm (1787-1854, distinguished in *electrical* research), who however obviously did not feel quite sure of himself, for he did not fail to mention that his observations were not very trustworthy. He expressly confessed that he was by nature so unmusical that he had to speak of tones with no more assurance than "a blind person speaking of colors."

The fact that we are far from being able to hear always all the tones exactly as Ohm thought we should, has been briefly discussed in Chapters XI and XII under the term "masking," although the emphasis in those chapters has been more on showing how the cochlea succeeds in *abating* masking than on showing when complete masking of higher tones is unavoidable.

In addition to tonal analysis the cochlea is responsible for the tones of Tartini. It also gives us both kinds of beats, multiple frequency beats as well as unison beats.

It is obvious that, in case the phragma of the cochlea is destroyed by an inflammatory disease, which happens occasionally, total deafness results, since the sensitive cells, the little microphones, are then destroyed, too. A more common kind of deafness is a reduction of loudness of tone and of that irregular mixture of brief tones which we call noise. It comes about through progressive hardening, "ossification" as the anatomists say, of the membranes closing the cochlear windows. Naturally no such movements of the liquid in the cochlea can occur, as described in Figures 3 and 4, while there are no *flexible* "window panes." The ossification begins sometimes in later childhood, sometimes in middle-age, sometimes in senility. As it progresses, the loudness of anything audible become weaker and weaker. The only advisable remedy in such cases is to make the physical sounds, which send air puffs against the windows or hammer the skull, artificially stronger. Instruments which are called "hearing aids," and which accomplish this artificial strengthening of the effects of physical sounds on the sense organ, are prescribed by physicians and are on sale in all large cities.

In rarer cases the ossification begins while the foetus is still in the mother's womb. An important medical discovery of recent years is that the foetus is in danger of suffering ossification of the cochlea windows when the pregnant mother, unaware of the consequences, takes a very strong dose of quinine in order to relieve a temporary suffering of her own. Pregnant women therefore ought to abstain from quinine. But in some cases deafness is hereditary in a family (also commonly in "albino" cats and dogs) in the sense that the unborn foetus without any other cause suffers a beginning ossification of the windows which soon after birth may become so pronounced that a high degree of deafness results in early childhood.

* * * * *

BIBLIOGRAPHY OF MOST SIGNIFICANT REFERENCES CONCERNING THE MECHANISM OF THE COCHLEA:

Archiv fur die gesamte Physiologie, 78, 1899, 357-362. *Ibid.* 81, 1900, 68-70.
The Psychology of the Other-One, The Missouri Book Company, Columbia, Missouri, 1921. Chapter 13, 294-312.
Journal of General Psychology, 1, 1928, 239-265.
Annals of Otology, Rhinology and Laryngology, 41, 1932, 323-331.
American Journal of Psychology, 63, 1950, 269-277.

Chapter XIX

THE GREATEST DISCOVERY IN MUSIC

The greatest discovery in music was made quite independently by innumerable tribes of mankind on earth thousands of years ago. This is the fact that when a person sings a tune and notices a desired succeeding tone to be out of range of his voice, a certain tone of totally different pitch can be substituted without in any conspicuous way interfering with the melody intended. The pitch which is successfully substituted may be much lower or much higher than the one which the singer could not produce. When physical science developed it was experimentally determined that the air wave frequencies of the two tones had the ratio 1:2, or even 1:4, and many attempts were made to explain the psychological effect mentioned. But these attempts were mostly speculative-metaphysical. It is now virtually certain that this effect results from a chemical property of the nervous system, the brain, which however thus far is only somewhat vaguely known. When one remembers that the nervous system is a vast network of electro-chemical conducting fibers, called neurons after the German anatomist, Waldeyer (1890), an explanatory idea like the following suggests itself. While one of the two serial electron charges of such and such a frequency ratio is conducted through certain neurons, the *conductivity* of these particular neurons may be more than ordinarily *favorable* during the same time and even a short time later for the serial electron charges of the other frequency. If that should be true, the melodious affinity between the two tones becomes plausible.

Around the year 600 A.D. Pope Gregory the Great extended his interests also over the practice and the teaching of music. He ordered the monks, who at that time were the organists as well as the teachers of church music, to call by a *single name* all the tones the frequency ratio of which is formed by 1 and a number being either 2 or 2 multiplied once or several times with itself. This whole kind of numbers is called in arithmetic "powers of 2;" therefore we shall henceforth call the numbers like 1, 2, 4, 8, 16, etc. by the generic name "a power of 2."

The number of tones used in church organs was not very great at that time, not as great as nowadays; and when the monks executed the order of the Pope, they found that they needed now for their own purposes only seven *names* for all the (more numerous) tones used, that is, the *first seven letters* of the alphabet, a, b, c, d, e, f, g. Any tone which formed with another tone, say d, a ratio among those just mentioned was also called d. The result of all this was that any combination of two tones of the frequency ratio 1:2 or 1:4 or 1:8 etc. was called by the Latin term "octava," which literally means "the eighth letter" but in practice means "seven letters are enough." Such is the origin of the curious name "octave," which we shall have to use frequently, simply because it has long been adopted by all the modern languages of the western world.

During the following centuries the number of tones within an octave span used for melodies increased and led to cumbersome practices of tuning instruments. Long continued experiments of organ tuners ended around 1700 with the conviction widespread among musicians that the most practical manner of tuning organs as well as all other musical instruments was that of dividing every single octave span into twelve exactly equal parts. This conviction was still further strengthened by the favor it received from the musical genius, Sebastian Bach (1685-1750), so that nowadays it has become musical practice without exception.

Some little explanation may be given in order to make arithmetically clear what is meant by twelve equal parts of an octave. As we mean by a single octave a frequency ratio 1:2, a twelfth part of it must mean that the *ratio* from the tone 1 to the next higher tone is exactly the same as the ratio from the latter to the next, and so forth; so that the twelfth ratio from the twelfth tone to the thirteenth (that is, to the octave tone 2) is again exactly the same as the other eleven ratios.

These twelve equal ratios can be computed. Their numerical value is 1000:1059. This is technically called the interval or "span" of a true chromatic "semitone." Still more correctly one should say "a *true enough* chromatic semitone." If we compute further decimals, they would have to be added after 1059; but that serves no sensible purpose. The first ratio up from the tone 1 is 1:1.059. When we multiply twelve factors 1.059 with one another, we get the tone 2, as proposed. Let us add a warning to the reader. These values are mentioned only for curiosity's sake. For the understanding of what follows in this book it is entirely superfluous to memorize or ever to return to this number 1059. On the other hand, the term "semitone" we shall meet again frequently, meaning thereby a twelfth of an octave span in the very sense in which this term would be used by Sebastian Bach if we could call his spirit and converse with him.

CHAPTER XX

THE TWO ASPECTS OF A MELODY: PITCH CHANGES AND MELODIOUS AFFINITIES

As the *frequency* of air pressure waves is varied, the pitch sensation is varied. The Ancient Greeks called that a change of "oxy'tes," which means *sharpness, acuteness*. The languages of the western world have only during the last few centuries adopted speaking of high frequencies as *high* tones and of low frequencies either as *low* or, more rarely, as deep tones. These terms are psychologically not well chosen. High suggests altitude above the ground, and that of course has no literal meaning for tones perceived. Low not only suggests close to the ground but — worse — may also suggest a low degree of loudness of the sensation, which is not meant here. Yet we can not avoid these terms.

A variation of pitch has psychological effects which are the same in music as in speech. The "inflection of the voice" is rightly emphasized in those books on speaking which used to be called "rhetoric" or "elocution." The emotional effects of pitch variation in music are identical with its psychological effects in speech. Attention is drawn to the lower pitch as if it were the answer to a question. The change from a lower to a higher pitch seems like asking a question and produces an expectative attitude. The multitudinous smaller changes affect the listener pleasantly as if he were looking at a mosaic or an oriental rug. Nothing further will be said about these effects in this book.

The second aspect of melody will be discussed here in some detail. That there is a strong affinity between tones of the frequency ratio 1:2 has already been brought out in the preceding chapter. The same neuro-chemical condition which was mentioned there applies also to ratios in which the numerical terms are, in addition to 1 and 2, the prime numbers 3, 5 and 7. The only difference is that where the numbers 3, 5 and 7 are combined among one another or combined with a power of 2, the affinity is much weaker than when a power of two is combined with another power of 2. Only in the latter case, $2^n:2^n$, can one indulge in accepting *melodious identity* of tones; in the former combinations there is merely a kind of family relationship, which we call *melodious affinity of the lower degrees*. But this does not mean that these lower degrees of affinity do not have a remarkable psychological effect, for otherwise music would not exist. Music consisting only of octave tones is unthinkable; it would lack enough variety.

A heckler might here ask the question: "Why stop at the prime number 7? Why not go beyond 7 and theorize with such prime numbers as 11, 13, 17, 19, etc?" The answer is that in Science one does not complicate theories beyond the necessity of understanding what is seen or heard or otherwise perceived. The sensory facts of music do not call for higher prime numbers. Before the time when the famous mathematician, Euler (1707-1783), showed the need of using it, even the prime number 7 was rejected by the musical theorists. But the need of going beyond 7 has not been shown by any scientists.

Of course, a melody will hardly ever be composed of only two tones differing in pitch. When there are more tones, often a dozen or two dozen different pitches in modern compositions, it is well to avoid naming them by means of the tiresome method of selecting a reference tone, often called "tonic", and then citing the ratio of that first with a second, the ratio of the same first with a third, the ratio of the first with a fourth tone and so forth; in spite of the fact that such a cumbersome method of putting down so many ratios, i. e., *fractions,* is terribly common in books on musical theory, we avoid it. A far better way is to state the relations of *all* the tones of the melody in a *single* but multiple ratio. That is done here below at once in a sample case.

48: 64: 75: 80: 96: 112.

Such a multiple ratio running from lower to higher frequencies could be called "the scale of the melody." That this "scale" begins with 48 as the lowest "rung of the ladder" is utterly irrelevant. You can begin it with any other of the numbers. That 48 stands on the left does not indicate that the writer wished to regard 48 as the most important of all the tones. The composer may emphasize in his music any tone he wants to and make it the principal tone psychologically. How he does that is his business as a composer.

48:      64: 75: 80: 96:   112:

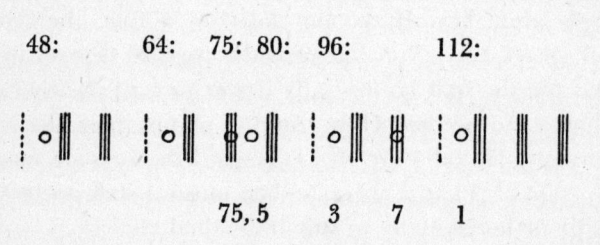

75, 5   3   7   1

Fig. 18. A sample of a musical scale. The bottom numbers are preferable, since they are easier to operate arithmetically.

We follow the advice of Pope Gregory and name octave tones only by a *single* name. That means the tones 48 and 96 should drop one of their names. A little thinking makes it still further clear that *even* numbers are *never* wanted in the description of a scale. Any even number which we come across in the preliminary statement must be divided by 2, and by 2 again and again until we reach the odd number which is the significant factor involved. We are as consistent as Pope Gregory and replace 48 (and 96) by 3, 64 by 1, 80 by 5 and 112 by 7. See Figure 18.

Now we need a "musical notation" for informing the person who plays the instrument. We reject the traditional musical notation and staff (dating from the *eleventh* century) as utterly antiquated for the music of the twentieth century, unnecessarily encumbered with so-called "flats" and "sharps" and what-nots. In Figure 18 we see a series of vertical *staff lines, five for the span of an octave,* each line a triplet only for conspicuity in the figure. The five triple lines represent the five *black keys of the piano keyboard* with which every musician is familiar. The location of the *white* keys among the black is obvious beyond further talk. The *dots* mark the keys *to be used.* If the *dot* falls on a white space, the "note" means a white key. If the dot falls on a line, the "note" means a black key. (You can turn the page 90 degrees to the left and use the staff horizontally if you prefer.) Neither flats nor sharps are needed. How could a pianist play sharps or flats anyway? He can only play keys. And the keys are marked by the "notes." That is an up-to-date musical staff, to be used vertically or horizontally to suit individual choice.

We follow the advice of Pope Gregory and do *not repeat the names* of the tones (numerically) if we only want to discuss "a scale." Therefore the lower series of numbers in Figure 18, having dropped either 96 or 48 and reduced the even numbers, is preferable to the upper series. That does not prevent the pianist-composer from striking the identical keys in the lower and higher octaves whenever he wishes. Of course, if as a composer he wishes to *tell another player* to strike those upper or lower octave tones, he will extend the staff of Figure 18 in either of the two possible directions as needed.

The bottom numbers of Figure 18 could as well be written beginning on the left with 1 and ending on the right with 7. The reason why we choose to begin with 75 and end with 1 is simply this. We want to guard against the false idea that 1, standing on the left, is by force the principal tone in this melody. Not so! Which tone the composer wants to make *the principal tone* is left to him to decide and to indicate by the manner in which he presents all the tones of the melody in his composition. It is his business to exert *psychological pressure* upon the hearer.

But now the inevitable question is left: *How did we know* that the (relative) tones 75, 5, 3, 7 and 1 (pitches rising in that order) are distributed over the twelve (relatively) possible keys in the *intervals* in which they appear in Figure 18 (leaving any possible *transposition* in absolute pitch to the choice of the player)?

For a quick and practical solution of the problem contained in the last question we use the little table of Figure 19, a square standing on one of its corners, the top meaning higher, the bottom lower pitches, the internal numbers giving us the span.

We may start with any of the tone numbers of our scale.

Let us start with 75. What is the interval, or "span" measured in semitones, or in "cents" which are so many one-hundredths of a semitone, from 75 going up to the frequency 5? We approach the answer in steps. From 75 going up to, say, 15 would be (the same as going from 15 up to 3 or as) going from 5 up to 1. The table tells us that from 5 going up to 1 is a span of 814 cents. The second computational step then

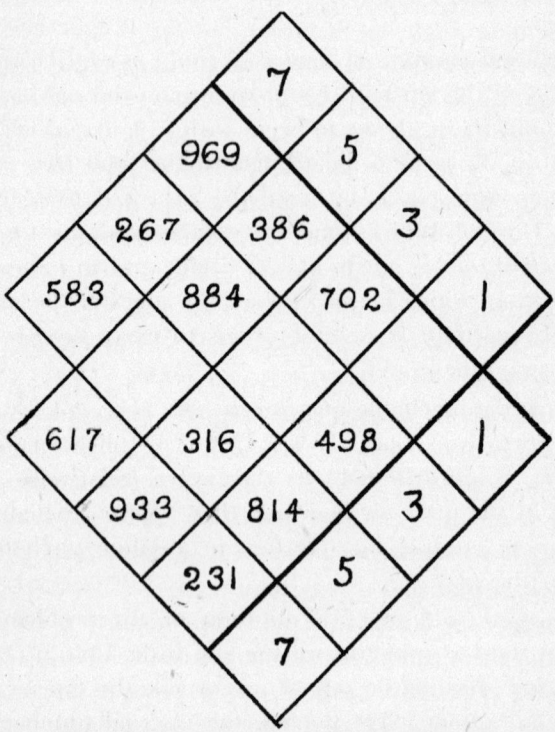

Fig. 19. Spans in cents between the combinations of the tones symbolized by 1, 3, 5 and 7 within one octave. Beyond one octave subtract multiples of "1200 cents."

94

is to go from 15 up to 5, which is the same as going from 3 up to 1.

The table tells us that this span is 498 cents. We add 498 to 814 and get 1312 cents. But 1200 cents are equal to 12 semitones, the exact span of an octave. Contrary to Pope Gregory's advice we have gone *outside* of the octave *limits*. Therefore we substract 1200 from 1312 and have 112 cents. That is the answer to the question. We observe that the span is a little more than one semitone but far distant from two semitones. Thus, when the musician plays out one semitone, the hearer has no difficulty in interpreting it to suit it melodiously with the other tones of this scale. It is true that 75 and 5 do not seem to be so closely affinitive that they can be treated like "blood-relatives," but they are certainly indirectly affinitive, call it affiliated like "relatives-by-marriage" through 45, 25 and 15, which in the hearer's past musical experience, through listening, have established the psychological bond. We know that musical appreciation does not appear spontaneously in full force in earliest childhood.

For a change, let us now start from the right side and ask what is the span of 1 going down to 7. The table tells us 231 cents. This is not very different from two semitones, but very different from one semitone and from three semitones. So the hearer has a chance to interpret it as the affinity between 1 and 7. It is true that it may require several hearings of the melody before the hearer interprets the composer as the latter desires. But there is nothing uncommon about that in musical history. We often have to hear a new piece of music many times before we feel inclined honestly to applaud the composer; sometimes we never do.

Going from 7 down to 3? The table tells us this is a span of

267 cents. We must play it out on the piano by using an interval of three semitones, as indicated in Figure 18.

Going from 3 down to 5? The table tells us this is a span of 316 cents or three semitones. But, remarks our heckler, going from 7 down to 3 was also a span of three semitones; how is the hearer to make an interpretative distinction? The answer was given in the second paragraph back above. The hearer often has to listen to a composer's work numerous times *before* he succeeds in interpreting the music as the composer intended; which is often equivalent to: *before he thoroughly enjoys the composer's work.* It is quite possible that an individual hearer and an individual composer never establish this happy relation between them.

The scale of Figure 18 may be, is in fact likely to be a mere *part* of a much larger scale containing even so many frequency ratio terms that *all the twelve* keys located *within* the span of an octave have to be used by the pianist to execute the piece of music. That octave keys are at his disposal goes without any further repetition.

Chapter XXI

ANOTHER SAMPLE OF A MUSICAL SCALE

A scientifically acceptable definition of a musical scale is this: *A scale is the sum total of all the tones* which a composer *has used* in a unitary piece of music; with the understanding, of course, that this unitary piece may be a part, a subdivision, of a much larger work such as an opera, for example. To this definition of a scale must also be added the proviso of Pope Gregory that octave tones should have only one naming representative, which proviso naturally signifies also that *the scale* thus defined can be and is confined within the limits of a single octave span.

Nevertheless, theoretically and even practically, nothing can force a composer to abstain from saying to himself, "These tones and no others are the ones which *I am going to* incorporate in my composition." For such a composer his scale would exist first and his composition would come afterwards. Historians well know that medieval composers usually followed such a rule of procedure in composing; they had traditionally fixed scales, but they were mostly pedants and not musical geniuses. Even so late and so capable a composer as Rameau (1683-1764) could not free himself from the notion that what in his opinion was the "real" scale consisted of only seven tones, and that to beget additional tones the "real" scale had to go through a process of child-bearing which was called "modulation."

Since this book is not devoted to teaching anybody how to compose artistic music, but only to understanding music theoretically, we are privileged to write down scales for discussion without any obligation of deriving them first from particular, published and thus already existing pieces of music.

The sample scale discussed in the preceding chapter was executed by *only five keys* of the keyboard, following the rule of Pope Gregory which restricts the number of *names* by excluding octaves. Let us now discuss a sample in which *all the twelve* keys are needed for execution, and the tones, although located within one octave, are even more than twelve.

216:225:240:243:252:270:288:300:320:324:336:360:384:400:405

The above is such a promised scale put down in the sensible way of *avoiding* any statement of so many *fractions* formed by one artificially chosen principal tone as numerators with each of the other tones as denominators. The inconvenience of that method, (here avoided), we have already pointed out in the preceding chapter. The above scale is written down as a *single multiple ratio,* which includes all the frequencies at once. At a first glance this multiple ratio looks as truly formidable as if its comprehension required that the reader be a natural "lightning calculator." However, that is so only because we have thus far neglected the advice of Pope Gregory that we ought not to worry about octave positions of pitch. That worry is gone as soon as we get rid of the even numbers through dividing every even number successively by 2 until we have arrived at *the odd numbers* which alone are *significant* for us here in theory. After having done this we have the identical multiple ratio below, which is composed of *numerical names* with which we are far *more familiar* from ordinary experiences with business arithmetic, although in modern music they must be *more than the medieval seven* (compare Chapter XIX).

27: 225: 15: 243: 63: 135: 9: 75: 5: 81: 21: 45: 3: 25: 405
3^3 $3^2 \cdot 5^2$ $3 \cdot 5$ 3^5 $3^2 \cdot 7$ $3^3 \cdot 5$ 3^2 $3 \cdot 5^2$ 5 3^4 $3 \cdot 7$ $3^2 \cdot 5$ 3 5^2 $3^4 \cdot 5$

In order to fit this scale into the piano keyboard, it is necessary to compute the span in cents (hundredths of a semitone) with the aid of the table given in the preceding chapter. The result of the computation will be given farther below without the computation itself being carried out here except in three instances which might cause the reader a little trouble.

First, the span between 15 and 243 is easily found as follows if we choose suitable steps. We go from 15 up to 3. This is identical with going from 5 up to 1; and the table gives us 814 cents. Now from 3 up to 243 is the same as making the step from 1 up to 3 four times ($3 \cdot 3 \cdot 3 \cdot 3 = 243$). Thus we have to add 702 four times, a total of 2808. This added to the 814 cents gives us 3622 cents. Now we have run up into multiple octaves, which in theory was forbidden by Pope Gregory. We subtract three octaves, that is, three times 12 semitones, or 3600 cents. Our quickly reached result is that going up from 15 to 243 is a span of only 22 cents. Naturally therefore the scale tones 15 and 243 are not played out on different keys, but on one and the same key, which on one occasion has to be interpreted by the listener as 15, on another occasion as 243. If the listener is incapable of this varied interpretation of the same pitch given out by the piano, because of his greatly limited experience in hearing music, he is incapable of understanding the composer—which is just too bad! It can not be helped, for no factory building pianos can provide more than twelve equally tempered intervals per octave, as was admitted by so great a genius as Sebastian Bach.

Second, the span between 5 and 81 can be found immediately when we notice that it must be the same as the span between 15 and 243, since the numbers 15 and 243 are simply the numbers 5 and 81 when each is multiplied with 3. So this span is also 22 cents. And the case of 25 going up to 405 is again analogous, only that the multiplying factor to 5:81 is 5 instead of 3. Thus the span between 25 and 405 is also 22 cents. The musical theorist meets *only a few* of these larger odd numbers in all his experience and soon learns to operate them, since the prime factors are restricted to 3, 5 and 7.

Third, let us determine the span between 63 and 135. From 63 going down to 9 is the same as going from 7 down to 1. The table gives us 969 cents. From 9 going up (we could also proceed using the table going down) to 27 is the same as going from 1 up to 3, for which we get from the table 702 cents. Thus from 63 down to 9 and up again to 27 means a step of 969 minus 702, or 267 cents down. From 27 down to 135, is the same as going from 1 down to 5; the table gives us 814 cents. These added to 267 gives 1081 cents *down*. Since in the scale 135 is *above* its neighbor in pitch 63, we rather go *up* to get from 63 to 135 the *narrower* span; all we have to do is to subtract 1081 from a full octave, from 1200 cents. Thus we know that going from 63 up to 135 covers a span of 119 cents, which on the piano is a semitone difference.

There are so many ways of procedure when one does not deal directly with prime numbers but with products of them, that no general advice can be given as to how to proceed. The computer must suit his individual liking and judgment as to what is most convenient to him. The result is the same, provided that we always subtract octaves, i. e., 1200 or a multiple of 1200 cents whenever we have arrived beyond the limits of the one octave within which we originally located our scale.

Let us give another example and let us now choose always to go up, never to go down in that table. Suppose we want to know how far we go from 21 up to 45. Now from 21 to 3 is in accordance with the table 231 cents. From 3 to 9 is 702. From 9 to 45 is 386. The sum of 231, 702 and 386 is 1319. Subtracting the octave 1200 leaves 119. So this is the step we want to know.

Now on the next page let us write down again our scale for greater convenience in a standing column. And on the right let us put all the successive spans so that we can see where all the tones belong on the keyboard. The *brackets* mean a single key serving several tones of the numerical scale. The third column repeats the prime factors composing the numbers.

This scale, which we selected by chance and not as an exclusive example, is served by *twelve* keys; that is, all the keys which we find in an octave span on the piano are needed, and several keys must serve in more capacities than one.

For a simple *proof of the computations* we should add all the spans. If we find a deviation from 1200 which amounts only to 1 or 2 cents, that does not signify incorrectness, for the spans in the table of Figure 19 for the prime numbers 1, 3, 5 and 7 have no decimals for cents but only rounded cents. An addition of many spans, therefore, must be expected to be often slightly different from what one would get if decimals were given in the table.

Spans between tones of a sample scale.

		cents	
High octave tone	27		3^3
		112	
same key {	405		$3^4 \cdot 5$
	25	22	5^2
		60	
	3		3
		112	
	45		$3^2 \cdot 5$
		119	
	21		$3 \cdot 7$
		63	
same key {	81		3^4
	5	22	5
		112	
	75		$3 \cdot 5^2$
		70	
	9		3^2
		112	
	135		$3^3 \cdot 5$
		119	
	63		$3^2 \cdot 7$
		63	
same key {	243		3^5
	15	22	$3 \cdot 5$
		112	
	225		$3^2 \cdot 5^2$
		70	
Low octave tone	27		3^3

And the scale is repeated without limits both above and below.

There are then for this particular scale three keys on the keyboard which have to serve the composer-pianist in a double sense. The listener to the music has to make the proper interpretation whenever one of these three keys is struck by the pianist. However, no extra difficulty is caused thereby, since the listener has to make the proper interpretation in all other cases, too. The tempered twelve-tone scale of the piano and of all other musical instruments has been approved, not only by Sebastian Bach, but by virtually all other great composers after him. The burden placed upon the listener is unavoidable unless we abolish all modern artistic music and restrict ourselves to music simple as a bugle call. The psychological burden placed upon the listener has been found in the experience of centuries as not being so great.

Chapter XXII

FROZEN MELODIES. SYMPHONIC MUSIC. THE POSSIBILITIES OF QUARTERTONES

In the Smithsonian Institution in Washington there are stored innumerable phonograph records of songs of North American Indians. It is not difficult to determine the numerical scale of each of these songs in the manner in which scale samples have been given in the two preceding chapters. There are no biologically *fundamental* differences in the music of our Western civilization, the music of the Indians just mentioned, the music of Asiatic peoples or of any other human beings on earth. It is all governed by the same neurological laws which are inherent in the human nervous system. Differences, surprising at a first acquaintance, are superficial as soon as they are sufficiently studied by historical and scientific methods. The main difference between the songs of the North American Indians and the songs which we hear in our homes, on our streets, in churches, in concert halls, etc., lies in the fact that we are accustomed to hear our songs with an "accompaniment." That is, we usually hear with each syllable not only (as in the Indian's song) a single tone, but two or three or more tones produced by instruments or by further human voices, a "chorus" as we say. Our cochlea, as we have shown in the earlier chapters, enables us to perceive several pitches at the same time; and our brain, though in a way only vaguely understood, enables us to interpret the various *melodious affinities* not only of successive but also of simultaneous tones.

That mankind during thousands of years of *primitive* civilizations used only the *successive* melodious affinities is so natural that it requires hardly a mentioning. But finally the mental limitation was overcome and the same melodious affinities were discovered to be perceivable in simultaneous tones. Omitting here the octave, it is self-evident that the possibility of melodiousness in simultaneous tones was discovered first with the two somewhat higher degrees of affinity which we referred to in previous chapters by the reduced ratio terms 1 combined with 3 and 1 combined with 5. A little later the combination of 3 with 5 was admitted into these "frozen melodies" as we may call them, because they lacked the liquidity of succession. Very much later, after about a thousand years of acquaintance with frozen melodies, the combinations 1 with 7, 3 with 7, and 5 with 7 were tried out by adventurous musicians and found to be admissible.

During the Middle Ages endless and useless debates occupied musical theorists with attempts to *classify* frozen melodies—or "chords, harmonies, consonances, fusions", etc., as they were then called—into good ones, better ones and worse ones. In the twelfth century a five-fold distinction became popularized: (1) perfect consonances, (2) fair consonances, (3) imperfect consonances, (4) imperfect dissonances, (5) perfect dissonances. It is like classifying human behavior into heroic conduct, good deeds, unmoral actions, moderate offenses and horrible crimes. The great composers of the twentieth century have thrown all these ridiculous classificatory attempts over board. They now use any melody of three, four, five, etc., tones, picked from any scale similar to that sampled in Chapter XXI, as a frozen melody or chord making the tones appear simultaneously; and they have won the approval of the musical public.

It is known that as early as the tenth century singers began to combine *two long melodies* so that they were heard at least to some length simultaneously. In the eleventh century Italian singers were especially venturesome, even in churches, through combining a rather stately song or sacred hymn of a slightly lower voice with a lively song, even a drink or love song, of a higher voice. This was called "discant." From these methods developed after many centuries of musical experimenting, the fugue; in it were combined usually four melodies, being essentially the same, but lying in different octaves or being at least transposed in pitch, so that the same melody started while the other one, or the other ones, were still in progress.

Organ fugues were especially developed by Sebastian Bach. But gradually fugues, also called "polyphonic" music, became slightly monotonous to the listeners; and the "symphonic" style prevailed in which varied melodies appeared without being similar to one another, simultaneously and successively entering at the composer's artistic fancy, with no restrictions to the nature of the resulting "chords" except the composer's own judgment. If the composer can not win the approval of the listening public, so much the worse for him personally. That, however, is exactly as it ought to be. There must be freedom from the dictation by theorists caught in the meshes of traditionalism.

If one should conclude from the uses which we have made of the table of "spans" in Figure 19 that the "twelve-tone and equally tempered" division of an octave permits the musician to take care of *all the products* of the factors 1, 3, 5 and 7, it would be too hasty a conclusion. In a very few cases which we shall discuss presently the cycle-frequency does not lie close enough to one or the other of two adjoining tones of a well tuned piano or organ to make the interpretation by the listener *easy enough*. Of course, after hearing the composer's music many, many times, the listener may finally succeed in interpreting the pitches given by the keys of the piano to agree with the ratio terms intended for his perception by the composer. If, however, there is a way of making the interpretation easier and more certain, why not use that way in tuning pianos, organs and other musical instruments? But what is it?

The solution of this problem naturally would require having more than twelve tones within the octave in tuning the instrument. Suggestions toward this end have often been made, but most of them are either *impractical* because they require *too many keys* (four or five times as many) of the keyboard, or utterly *impossible* because they insist on throwing away all the advantages of the *twelve-tone* division. For example, the idea of replacing the twelve divisions by eighteen equally tempered divisions is of the latter kind. If we want more tones, we ought to pass from using twelve to using twenty-four; provided we construct a keyboard so that it is easy to neglect, in playing, the twelve additional (and vertical!) keys and use only the twelve original ones.

Let us look for products of the ratio terms 1, 3, 5 and 7 which might call for additional tones on the piano. Really, the only likely products of this kind are 35 and products of 35 multiplied with 3 or, maybe, with 5. Let us compute with the help of our table of Figure 19 the span of 35 going up to

9. The first step may be from 35 to 7, which is the same as 5 to 1. The table gives us 814. The second step is from 7 to 1. The table gives us 231. The third step is from 1 to 3. The table gives us 702. From 3 to 9 this same step is repeated, 702. Adding the four spans we get 2449 cents. We subtract 2400 cents because that is the equivalent of two octaves. We know then that the tone 35 lies right in the middle of a semitone interval, 49 cents from one tone of the piano, 51 cents from the other tone of the piano. This example will suffice to make clear the advantage to the composer, the player, the listener if tones are available which lie almost exactly *in the middle* between two ordinary tones of the piano.

Since the originally adopted and *literal* meaning of "semitone" is "half-tone" (although this historical meaning serves no good purpose nowadays), we might very well choose to call the resulting 24 equally tempered intervals of the piano "quartertones." That is nothing, of course, but a convenient name; and any other name might serve just as well as soon as everybody understands what we mean thereby.

Two designs have been published of keyboards which will serve both to preserve the present and ordinary keyboard and to add the twelve additional keys without interfering with the original twelve. The reader who is interested in seeing these keyboard designs may find pictures of them in the present author's book, *The Musician's Arithmetic,* which, first published by the University of Missouri, is obtainable from the music publisher, Theodore Presser (Bryn Mawr, Philadelphia, Pennsylvania). One of these designs is by the German musician, Moellendorff. The other is by the present writer. The reader may compare there the advantages or disadvantages of each and take his choice or reject both.

There is quite a difference of opinion, nevertheless, between Moellendorff and Meyer. The former believes that quartertones should be used very freely in connection with semitones, almost as freely as the semitones themselves. Meyer believes that semitones almost alone will be usually sufficient even for the composer of a symphony; but that *occasionally* the composer may want to produce an effect (like "35" above) which he can *not decisively* produce without one or two of these additional tones, here and there, in his composition. The reader should also be aware of the fact that the use of quartertones does not imply that *so small intervals* as quartertones must actually appear in a composition. This would be as untrue as expecting a composer in a composition on the ordinary piano always to make continuous runs from semitone interval to semitone interval and so forth to the next and the next. Let us remember that on the ordinary piano we often play a song in which so small an interval as a semitone rarely appears.

He who even merely suggests to the composer to experiment with quartertones, lays himself open to this legitimate challenge: Can you give an example of a striking advantage accruing to the composer who uses a quartertone instrument? The following proposal made in my book which is mentioned two paragraphs back might be accepted as meeting this demand. A very ordinary esthetic device used by composers is "variations" of a theme by exchanging "minor" and "major" as the musicians say, or in plainer language by varying one pitch of the theme by a semitone. The quartertone instrument makes a *third variation* easily possible if judiciously used.

Let us examine Figure 20. In example A as in example B, the two variations I and III can be executed on the common piano. But the variations II in A and B, lost to the composer who depends on the common piano, can be executed only on an instrument tuned in quartertones and having the quartertone keyboard. In Figure 20 the *arrowheads* pointing down indicate lowering the pitch by a quartertone.

In order to demonstrate that those under II are real variations we write the numerical scales below; first the one for A.

a	b♭	↓b	b	c	e	f	a♭
15	63	525	135	9	45	3	7, 225
$3 \cdot 5$	$3^2 \cdot 7$	$3 \cdot 5^2 \cdot 7$	$3^3 \cdot 5$	3^2	$3^2 \cdot 5$	3	$7, 3^2 \cdot 5^2$

It is to be noted that a♭ requires a double interpretation by the hearer, as 7 in the case I, as 225 in the cases II and III.

Fig. 20. Three variations of a theme, made possible by a quartertone instrument, instead of ony two variations. The staff is explained in Figure 18 and in the next chapter. The arrowhead pointing downward indicates lowering the pitch by a quartertone.

Now the numerical scale for B.

a	b♭	↓b	b	c	e♭	e	a♭
15	63	525	135	9	21	45	7, 225
$3 \cdot 5$	$3^2 \cdot 7$	$3 \cdot 5^2 \cdot 7$	$3^3 \cdot 5$	3^2	$3 \cdot 7$	$3^2 \cdot 5$	7, $3^2 \cdot 5^2$

Here again it is to be noted that a♭ requires a double interpretation by the hearer, as 7 in the case I, as 225 in the cases II and III. That kind of requirement made on the hearer is commonplace in modern music.

If we return again to the keyboard problem: the *mechanical* problem has been virtually solved; the problem left is one of choice by the owner of the instrument. *Must* he have his piano tuned in twelve-tone divisions? Or may he be permitted (if he can pay for it) to tune it, properly built, in twenty-four tone divisions? In either case it is left to the composer to use only a limited number of the twelve equally tempered tones or a limited number of the twenty-four equally tempered tones!

Chapter XXIII

A RATIONAL SCRIPT FOR MUSIC

Two thousand years back the tones of a melody were always written by the composer simply in the letters of the common alphabet. We have pointed out in Chapter XIX that Pope Gregory around the year 600 A.D. greatly simplified the methods of putting down music in writing by ordering the clerics to name all "octave" tones by identical letters. Music then *traditionally* used only *seven* pitches within the span of a single octave. The explanation of the origin of that tradition is not difficult and can be found in the above mentioned book, *The Musician's Arithmetic;* but it is elaborate and therefore beyond the scope of the present book. The seven pitches of the Greek and Roman theorizers and composers were distributed from *a* to the higher *a* as shown in the next two lines, the *approximate* intervals being there indicated.

a	b	c	d	e	f	g	(a)
two	one	two	two	one	two	(two)	semitones

It is at once clear from the above display that, when music in later centuries developed a more complex structure which used twelve pitches instead of seven, by obvious logic *five new names* were called for, to be added to the seven to which the Pope had wisely restricted his contemporary music writers.

Here then was the (regrettably missed) opportunity for rationally introducing five other letters of the alphabet, to be placed wherever in the above tabular lines the word "two" appears within the span from *a* to its higher octave *a*. The following line would have composed a clear nomenclature useful for the modern pianist, since *r* and *s* would have marked the *two* grouped black keys, and *x, y* and *z* would have marked the *three* grouped black keys:

a, z, b, c, r, d, s, e, f, x, g, y, (a)

Cultural progress rarely occurs in one great bound but comes drawn out over tiny steps, *retarded* by theoretical notions and vested interests, with frequently very unreasonable results. So it was here. The musicians did not fill all the five pitch vacancies at once. Perhaps a little before the year 1400 they filled the single vacancy between *a* and *b*. Even this they did not do because they desired to compose melodies by the use of eight pitches instead of the traditional seven. It actually came about in the following way. Occasionally the organist wanted to accommodate a singer by transposing the melody to a different absolute pitch, to fall within the voice range of the singer. Then, for reasons which no longer hold good, but which suited the prejudices of the epoch, he transposed either a "Fourth" upward or by a "Fifth" downward. Thus, what used to be sung on pitch *c* would now be sung on *f*. The next six lines show the comparison.

I. Keys painted   c   d   e   f   g   a   b   (c)
II. Interval spans   2S 2S S   2S 2S 2S S

III.	Original	c	d	e	f	g	a	b	(c)
IV.	Transposed	f	g	a	b	c	d	e	(f)
V.	Wrong intervals	2 S	2 S	**2 S**	**S**	2 S	2 S	S	

| VI. | Corrected | f | 'g | a | b♭ | c | d | e | (f) |

Thus a new key and an additional organ pipe were needed and introduced. The names from *a* to *g* were at that time *painted* on the keys as otherwise the organist would not have known which was which. The keys appear above in line I, the intervals in line II. The original melody here assumed is written in line III.

The transposed melody, as played in line IV, was heard to be wrong because the key *b* gave a pipe tone which was a semitone too high. So the organists helped themselves with a single *intermediate* key which was painted with a different looking *b,* a *round* letter. We must remember that the medieval monks *customarily* wrote the letters cornered, more or less *square,* as we still find inscriptions on old cathedrals in England and the Continent.

This new form of the letter *b,* nowadays round only above but pointed downwards, appears on our common music staff as the sign ♭ used *generalizingly* to indicate that any white key written on the staff should not be played, but the black key next, to the left, in its stead.

The opportunity of introducing five more *letter* names into the musical nomenclature was completely missed. When gradually all the other new (black) keys were introduced into the keyboard, an absurd tradition became foisted upon the musical world. The black keys assumed such names as b-flat, g-flat, etc.; still later even such names as f-sharp, gsharp, a-sharp, etc. To reach the climax of awkwardness, the folderol of talking of double-flats, double-sharps and naturals became common practice among musicians, supported by strong though obsolete theories. The wonder is that nobody has ever yet talked of triple-flats and triple-sharps, although there is no logical reason for abstaining from it if the other names are excused by (spurious) logical derivation.

Naming, in *reading* off, the tones of a melody is one thing; *writing* the melody is another. By the year 1000 musicians had found it inconvenient to write a melody by putting down the letters of the alphabet as the names for the relative pitches. They invented the *staff* writing which avoids the letters. At first only three staff lines were used and the notes were written with suitable vertical spacing among and above and below the three lines to suggest the various pitches. In order to increase the accuracy, Guido d'Arezzo (about 995-1050) accustomed the musicians to using a fourth line. After this improvement a fifth line was added. Thus the staff originated in which written music has come down far into the twentieth century. The abominable feature of this staff, intended only for the seven (white) keys, is the need of signs for "flats" or "sharps."

All those who during the last half-century have occupied themselves in a practical way with the problem of the music staff are in agreement on choosing five basic lines, but defined on a totally different principle from that of Guido d'Arezzo. These five lines are spaced exactly as the black keys are conspicuously spaced on the piano and organ keyboard. With this spacing of the *black keys* every reader of music and every writer of music is already familiar.

Figure 18 in Chapter XX shows that on such a staff all the

notes used in modern music can be written with ease and read off with ease without the need of all the confusing signs of flats, sharps and naturals which encumber the commonly printed music of the last four centuries. If quartertones should be wanted, lowering the pitch by a quartertone is easily indicated by a single sign, an *arrowhead pointing downward* as used in Figure 20. This keyboard staff can be used in two ways, either for writing music *horizontally*, left to right, or *vertically*, from above down. To illustrate the former way, Figure 18 should be turned ninety degrees to the left and the examples of Figure 20 should be compared. Many pieces of familiar music have been printed *horizontally on this staff* during the last quarter-century and are offered for sale by Robert B. Robinson in Kansas City, Missouri.

Although we Westerners are not accustomed to vertical writing of any kind as are the Chinese and Japanese, for the *player of music* the vertical printing of music makes the reading of it even easier than the horizontal printing, since he has the staff lines before him in exactly the same position in which he has the black keys of the piano before him. Thus he need not turn the page in his mind's eye, although even this turning by ninety degrees is quickly learned without any effort comparable to that of learning to read from the traditional staff with its confusing signs. The Dutch engineer, Cornelis Pot, has courageously invested much capital in printing thousands of pieces of the best existing music, both popular and classical, on the keyboard staff in *vertical printing*. He has called this method by a word of the Esperanto language "Klavarskribo." Music teachers of beginners should know that this printed music can be bought at a low price from the Klavarskribo Institute in Slikkerveer near Rotterdam, Netherlands. (American Klavarskribo Institute, Box 252, Decatur, Illinois.)

Another innovation which has been introduced by the Klavarskribo Institute is that of using only one form of notes instead of the enormous number of kinds which are ordinarily used to indicate the relative *length* of each tone. As a matter of fact the length of each note is only an indicator of the *rhythms* proposed by the composer. Both the virtuoso and the orchestra conductor take great liberties with the (mathematical) length of the notes as written on the staff in order to bring out the greatest esthetic effect by putting the tones together in the rhythm on which this maximal effect depends. In the music printing as used by the Klavarskribo Institute the rhythm is indicated essentially by the judicious placing of the notes within the measure, together with a few easily understandable marks. This method is entirely in accordance with the results of modern psychological investigations.

We look back at the beginning of this book. From discussing the shaking of a lead pipe filled with water to the physiological functioning of the cochlea may seem a big jump; and from the latter to frozen melodies and even quartertone music may seem another big jump. But without thinking of the lead pipe we could not have understood the functioning of the cochlea. And without having received from the cochlea the sensory ability to perceive a number of tones at the same time, mankind could not now be in possession of that great achievement, our modern music.

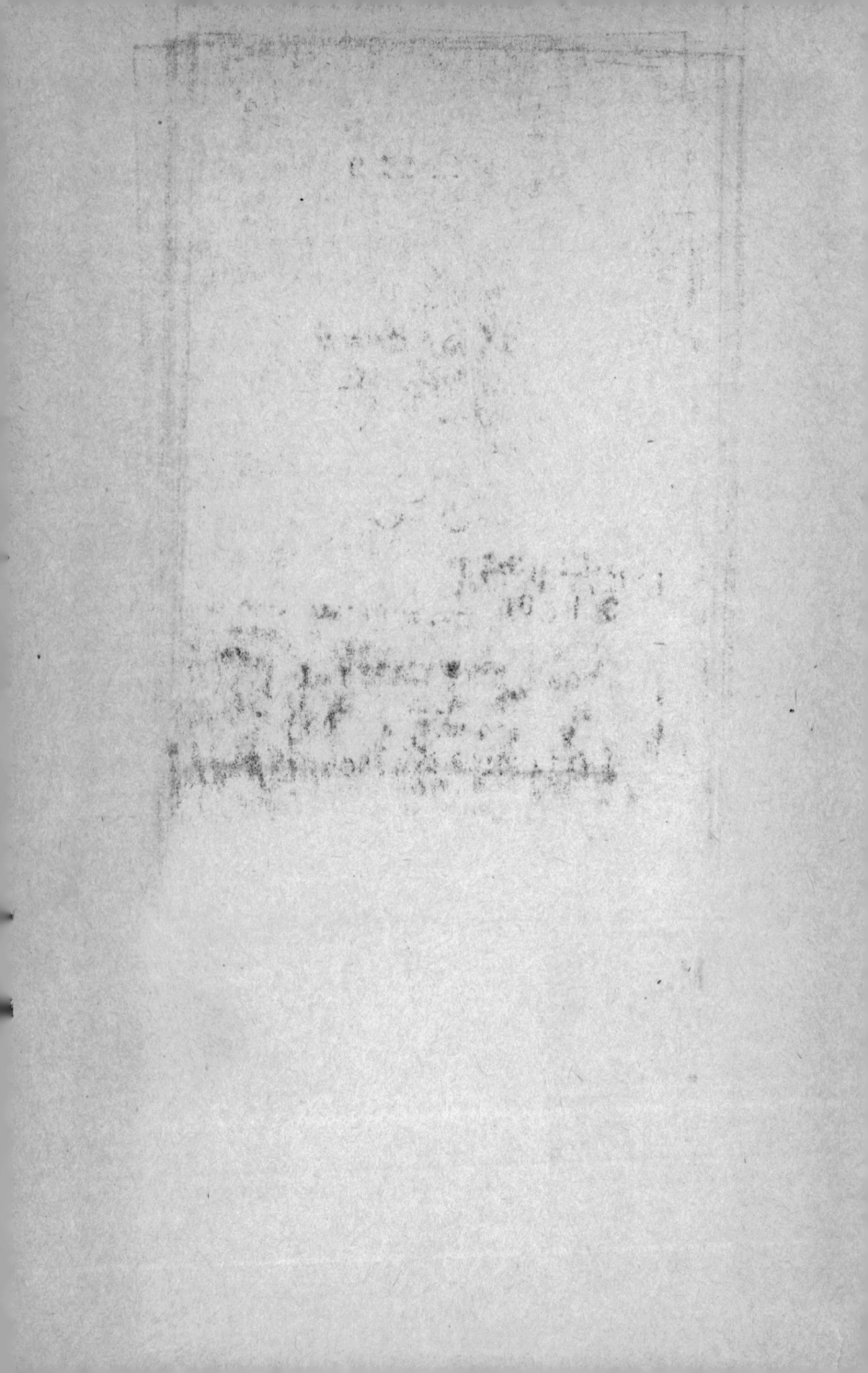